PANZER I
VS
SHERMAN

France 1944

STEVEN J. ZALOGA

OSPREY PUBLISHING
Bloomsbury Publishing Plc

Kemp House, Chawley Park, Cumnor Hill, Oxford OX2 9PH, UK
1385 Broadway, 5th Floor, New York, NY 10018, USA
Email: info@ospreypublishing.com

OSPREY is a trademark of Osprey Publishing, a division of
Bloomsbury Publishing Plc

First published in Great Britain in 2015 by Osprey Publishing

A CIP catalog record for this book is available from the British Library

Print ISBN: 978 1 4728 0760 1
PDF ebook ISBN: 978 1 4728 0761 8
ePub ebook ISBN: 978 1 4728 0762 5

Index by Rob Munro
Typeset in ITC Conduit and Adobe Garamond
Maps by bounford.com
Originated by PDQ Media, Bungay, UK
Printed and bound in India by Replika Press Private Ltd.

21 22 23   15 14 13 12 11 10 9 8 7

The Woodland Trust
Osprey Publishing supports the Woodland Trust, the UK's leading woodland
conservation charity.

www.ospreypublishing.com
To find out more about our authors and books visit our website. Here you will
find extracts, author interviews, details of forthcoming events and the option
to sign-up for our newsletter.

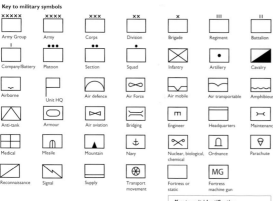

Acknowledgments
The author was pleased to interview Oberst aD Helmut Ritgen about his
wartime experiences at an "Art of War" Symposium sponsored by the US
Army at the *Kaserne* of 1. Gebirgs-Division in Garmisch-Partenkirchen in
1987. He was kind enough to answer further questions in correspondence over
the years. I would also like to thank Peter Brown for his generous help on
British tank data.

Author's note
Unless otherwise noted, all photographs are from the author's collection. For
brevity, the traditional conventions have been used when referring to units. In
the case of US units, H/66th Armored refers to Company H, 66th Armored
Regiment; 2/66th Armored refers to the 2nd Battalion, 66th Armored
Regiment. The US Army traditionally uses Arabic numerals for divisions and
smaller independent formations (4th Division, 741st Tank Battalion); Roman
numerals for corps (VII Corps), spelled numbers for field armies (First US
Army) and Arabic numerals for army groups (12th Army Group). In the case
of German units, 2./PzRgt 7 refers to 2. Kompanie, Panzer-Regiment 7; II./
PzRgt 7 indicates II. Abteilung, Panzer-Regiment 7. German corps are referred
to using Roman numerals (LXXXIV. Armeekorps), while German field armies
use Arabic numerals (e.g. 7. Armee).

Title-page photograph: Many PzKpfw IV and M4 tanks are preserved in
museums around the world. This view from Jacques Littlefield's Military
Vehicles Technology Museum in Portola Valley, California shows a PzKpfw IV
Ausf H next to an M4A1 prior to the museum being shuttered in 2013. Like
many of the preserved PzKpfw IV in museums, this was a former Syrian Army
tank that originally had been obtained in the 1950s from French, Spanish, and
Czechoslovak stocks. It was production serial 89457, produced by the
Nibelungenwerk in April 1944.

Glossary

Abt	*Abteilung* : German formation between battalion and regiment in size.
AFAB	armored field artillery battalion; equipped with M7 105mm HMC.
AFV	armored fighting vehicle; in World War II this term usually encompassed tanks, assault guns, and tank destroyers.
Ausf	*Ausführung* : variant.
CCA	Combat Command A, one of three combined-arms battlegroups in a US armored division (also CCB and CCR).
ETO	European Theater of Operations.
FJR	*Fallschirmjäger-Regiment* : German parachute regiment.
GMC	gun motor carriage; most often a tank destroyer.
GR	*Grenadier-Regiment* ; German infantry regiment.
Heer	the German Army.
HMC	howitzer motor carriage; an armored self-propelled field howitzer.
Kampfgruppe	German battlegroup of indeterminate size, usually in the battalion–regiment range.
Kampfwert	combat value.
KwK	*Kampfwagenkanone* : tank gun.
OB West	Oberbefehlshaber West: High Command West.
PzKpfw	*Panzerkampfwagen* : literally armored combat vehicle.
StuG	*Sturmgeschütz* : assault gun.
Wehrmacht	German armed forces: included Heer, Waffen-SS, Luftwaffe, Kriegsmarine.

CONTENTS

INTRODUCTION

This Osprey Duel title examines the two principal Allied and German tanks of the 1943–44 fighting, the PzKpfw IV and M4 Sherman. The PzKpfw IV was the older of the two designs, tracing its lineage back to the mid-1930s. It was originally intended as a fire-support tank to complement the main battle tank of the Panzer divisions, the PzKpfw III. This mission changed after Germany confronted the Red Army during Operation *Barbarossa* in the summer of 1941. The appearance of large numbers of Soviet T-34 and KV tanks was a technological shock to the Panzer force. These tanks were significantly better than the PzKpfw III in terms of armor, firepower, and mobility. As a short-term solution, the existing German tanks were modernized with better armor and better firepower. The PzKpfw III was inherently constrained by its narrow superstructure that prevented the adoption of a larger turret ring. This limited the power of the gun that could be fitted to the turret since a small turret ring could not endure the recoil forces of some of the newer tank guns. The PzKpfw IV had a wider superstructure and larger turret ring, and so was more easily adapted to more powerful versions of the 7.5cm tank guns. As a result, the PzKpfw IV shifted from being a supplementary tank in the Panzer divisions to being the principal battle tank. Use of the PzKpfw III gradually faded, and production of the chassis shifted from the tank version to the StuG III assault gun. The PzKpfw IV began to outnumber the PzKpfw III in service by July 1943.

The PzKpfw IV with the long 7.5cm guns underwent continual modification from the Ausf G in May 1942 to the Ausf J in February 1944. The focus of this Duel is the fighting in Normandy in July 1944, and so the variant at the heart of this discussion is the PzKpfw IV Ausf H, which was the main type in service with the Panzer divisions in France in the summer of 1944. In early June 1944, there were 758 PzKpfw IV tanks in the West out of the 2,387 in service. The PzKpfw IV remained the main battle tank

of the Wehrmacht through 1944. There had been hopes that the larger and more powerful Panther tank would take over this role. The Panther was first introduced in the summer of 1943 at the time of the battles of Kursk–Orel but proved to be a disappointment due to technical immaturity. By the summer of 1944, many of these problems had been overcome and the Panther offered significant advantages over the PzKpfw IV in terms of armor, firepower, and mobility. However, the Panther was more costly and time-consuming to manufacture. As a result, the 1944 Panzer regiments were based around a battalion of PzKpfw IV and a battalion of Panthers. The plan to replace the PzKpfw IV with the Panther never occurred due to the limitations of German war industries and the PzKpfw IV remained the most numerous German battle tank until August 1944, the first occasion when it was outnumbered in service by the Panther.

The M4 and M4A1 Sherman tanks were developed later than the PzKpfw IV, with initial production in February 1942. The Sherman was a lineal descendant of the M2 and M3 medium tanks. While it differed considerably in its armament layout from these earlier types, it was very similar in its automotive aspects including the engine and suspension. This long lineage helps to explain why the Sherman tank proved to be a dependable design from the very outset of production, and suffered few of the teething pains typically found in new tank designs. The arrival of the M4 Sherman roughly corresponded to the arrival of the first of the long-barreled PzKpfw IV, so the designs are not so widely separated as might first seem from their production histories. When the Sherman first debuted in combat at El Alamein in October 1942, it was

An M4A1 of F/33rd Armored (CCB, 3rd Armored Division) passes a knocked-out PzKpfw IV Ausf G, probably from 11. Panzer-Division, in Bad Marienberg on March 28, 1945, during the breakout from the Remagen bridgehead. This M4A1 is a survivor from the Normandy campaign and has a large steel plate added to the hull front, a modification on many 3rd Armored Division tanks following the capture of Köln earlier in the month.

The tank commander in the PzKpfw IV occupied the "throne" at the rear of the turret. An improved commander's vision cupola with the diameter increased by 100mm was introduced early in the production of the Ausf G in February 1943. The new cupola switched from a split hatch to a single-piece hatch as shown here. This is the PzKpfw IV Ausf H commanded by SS-Oberscharführer Johann Terdenge who led 2. Zug, 6./SS-PzRgt 12 (*Hitlerjugend* Division) while training near Ostend in Belgium during the winter of 1943/44. Another photograph here (on page 12) shows this same tank after its capture in July 1944.

widely regarded as the best Allied tank of the day. British tanks of the 1940–42 period had relied on the 2-pdr and 6-pdr guns which offered excellent antitank performance but poor high-explosive performance. Since the majority of tank combat involved the use of high-explosive ammunition, this was a significant drawback in combat. The American 75mm gun proved to be a more versatile weapon and became the commonest weapon on Allied tanks through the end of the war. The Sherman tank also enjoyed a reputation for excellent reliability, a very important feature in mechanized warfare and one that is often overlooked.

The Sherman design stagnated after its combat introduction in 1942–43. It continued to see combat use in the Mediterranean theater, facing the same mix of PzKpfw III and PzKpfw IV tanks that had been met in combat in North Africa and Tunisia. There were hints that the Panzer force was improving, with occasional encounters with the new Tiger tank. However, the limited number of tank-versus-tank encounters in the Mediterranean theater led to complacency in the US Army's armored force. Some steps were taken to develop a more powerful 76mm gun for the Sherman, but there was a surprising degree of reluctance to accept these into combat service. The

first batches of M4A1 (76mm) arrived in Britain in April 1944, but they were orphans for several months because none of the armored divisions wanted the inconvenience of adopting a new version with new logistics challenges. It is worth noting that the British commanders had a fundamentally different viewpoint, and had developed their own Sherman variant with the powerful 17-pdr gun to deal with anticipated German threats that would be faced after the D-Day landings. Besides the complacency over tank firepower, US tank units were surprisingly indifferent to the need for better armor on the Sherman tank.

This Duel examines the first large-scale tank-versus-tank fighting between US and German forces in Normandy during Operation *Cobra*, that began on July 25–26, 1944. This battle started with a confrontation between the US Army's 2nd and 3rd Armored divisions against three German Panzer and *Panzergrenadier* divisions and became the largest tank engagement fought by the US Army up to this point in the war. By the end of July 1944, the First US Army deployed four armored divisions and 13 separate tank battalions with a combined strength of 1,555 tanks, about one-third of them M5A1 light tanks, plus 880 tank destroyers, and several hundred other AFVs including self-propelled artillery and armored cars. During Operation *Cobra*, they faced fewer than 300 German tanks and assault guns along a frontage less than 30km wide. To put this in perspective, Operation *Cobra* involved more AFVs than the legendary tank battle of Prokhorovka during the Kursk campaign. During the key phase of the Prokhorovka battle on July 12, 1943, about 420 German and 840 Soviet tanks and assault guns were present on a 50km sector.

Prior to Normandy, the 2nd Armored Division saw its most prolonged combat action during Operation *Husky*, the amphibious assault on Sicily in July 1943. This M4A1 named *Eternity* of E/67th Armored is shown traversing the dunes shortly after landing at Gela at the start of the campaign.

CHRONOLOGY

1938
January First issue of the PzKpfw IV Ausf A to German troops.

1940
July 15 2nd Armored Division is activated at Fort Benning, Georgia.

1941
February Start of US development of T6 medium tank.

1942
February T6 accepted for service as M4A1 medium tank; production started at Lima Locomotive Works.

May Initial production of PzKpfw IV Ausf F2 (Ausf G) with long L/43 gun.

July Initial production of M4 medium tank at Pressed Steel Car Co.

October Combat debut of M4A1 (Sherman II) tank during the battle of El Alamein.

November Combat debut of M4A1 with US 2nd Armored Division during Operation *Torch* in French North Africa.

1943
April Initial production of PzKpfw IV Ausf G with long L/48 7.5cm KwK 40 gun.

May Initial production of PzKpfw IV Ausf H.

December Final production of M4A1 with 75mm gun.

December 30 OKH orders the activation of Panzer-Lehr-Division.

ABOVE During an interrogation in early July, a captured Panzer crewman from *Das Reich* mocked the US Army's negligent camouflage procedures. Prior to Operation *Cobra*, new camouflage routines were introduced. The 70th Tank Battalion as shown here fitted Sommerfeld matting to their tanks to facilitate the addition of foliage camouflage. Other units, including both 2nd and 3rd Armored divisions, confined their efforts to pattern-painted camouflage.

ABOVE Owing to the prevalence of Allied fighter-bombers, German tank crews maintained strict camouflage discipline. Foliage camouflage was widely used in Normandy, as in this case of a PzKpfw IV Ausf H of II./SS-PzRgt 12.

1944

January	Initial production of M4A1 with 76mm gun at Pressed Steel Car Co.
February	Start of production of PzKpfw IV Ausf J at Nibelungenwerk.
July 24	A false start of Operation *Cobra* when mission is canceled due to weather; some bombers attack anyway.
July 25	Start of Operation *Cobra*.
July 26	Initial commitment of 2nd and 3rd Armored divisions during Operation *Cobra*.
July 27	Panzer-Lehr-Division overrun and ineffective.
July 28/29	2. SS-Panzer-Division *Das Reich* begins to withdraw, igniting a series of night battles with 2nd Armored Division.
July 29/30	A second night of fighting between the retreating 2. SS-Panzer-Division *Das Reich* and 2nd Armored Division.

BELOW A set of side skirts (*Schürzen*) were added to the PzKpfw IV towards the end of Ausf G production to protect against Soviet antitank rifles. In many cases, the hull side skirts were left off since they hampered daily suspension maintenance. This is a Finnish PzKpfw IV Ausf J, one of 15 delivered in August 1944, pictured in Oulu, northern Finland on November 12, 1944. This overhead view provides a good impression of the shape of the turret skirt armor. This particular tank, Ps.221-6, is still preserved at the Finnish museum at Parola. (SA-Kuva)

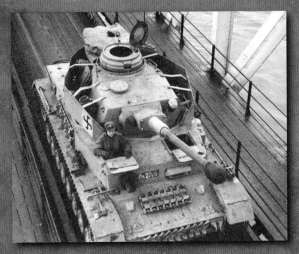

DESIGN AND DEVELOPMENT

PzKpfw IV

The PzKpfw IV was developed in the mid-1930s as one of a pair of new medium tanks for the German Army, the Heer. The ZW (*Zugführerwagen*, or "section commander's vehicle") was intended to be the principal battle tank and was armed with a 3.7cm gun and multiple machine guns; it eventually emerged as the PzKpfw III. The BW (*Bataillonsführerwagen*, or "battalion commander's vehicle") was armed with a short 7.5cm gun and was intended to be a fire-support tank to accompany the ZW to deal with fortified positions and other targets requiring greater high-explosive firepower. This eventually emerged as the PzKpfw IV. The Heer intended to manufacture the ZW/BW combination in roughly the same ratio of light to heavy machine guns in the infantry or roughly 4:1 in favor of the PzKpfw III. The origins of both the PzKpfw III and PzKpfw IV through the 1940 campaign are covered in greater detail in other Osprey Duel titles.[1]

The 1940 campaign in France and the Low Countries did not challenge the basic idea of a mix of two medium tanks, but it did highlight the need for better armor and better firepower on the PzKpfw III. The new PzKpfw III Ausf G received the 5cm KwK 38 L/42 and there were about 620 PzKpfw III with this gun taking part in

---

1 Steven Zaloga, *Panzer III vs Somua S 35: Belgium 1940* (Osprey Duel 63: 2014); *Panzer IV vs Char B1 bis: France 1940* (Osprey Duel 33: 2011).

Operation *Barbarossa*, the invasion of the Soviet Union in June 1941, or more than half of all PzKpfw III. The infantry adopted the 5cm PaK 38 and there were about 850 in service by the time of the invasion of the Soviet Union. In May 1941, there was some discussion of rearming the PzKpfw IV with the longer L/60 PaK 38 gun or an improved 7.5cm L/33 gun. Gun-barrel length is expressed in multiples of the bore caliber, so the 300cm length of the PaK 38 tube is expressed as L/60 (300cm = 5.0cm × 60). Barrel length has an important role in the performance of antitank guns since a longer tube allows the propellant a greater period of time to impart its energy to the projectile and increase its velocity. Velocity of the projectile is the key to armor penetration since the projectile energy on impact is equivalent roughly to half the square of the velocity times the projectile mass. The two guns used the same ammunition, but the L/42 had an initial muzzle velocity of 685m/sec and could penetrate 46mm of armor angled at 30 degrees at a range of 500m; the equivalent figures for the L/60 were 835m/sec and 58mm.

The Wehrmacht had seriously underestimated the Soviet tank threat and had not anticipated the deployment of the new T-34 medium tank or KV heavy tank. Both tanks employed an excellent dual-purpose 76mm gun and had much heavier armor than other Soviet or German tanks. The tank panic caused by the surprise appearance of these tanks led to several programs to improve German tank performance. In the long term, it prompted the development of the new Panther medium tank and Tiger heavy tank. In the short term it led to programs to improve the firepower of the

The PzKpfw IV Ausf F2, later designated as Ausf G, used a ball-shaped muzzle brake on its L/43 main gun. This example was captured by the US Army in Tunisia in early 1943 and is pictured at a display in Washington, DC in February 1944 with two US soldiers dressed in Deutsches Afrikakorps uniforms.

The PzKpfw IV began to outnumber the PzKpfw III in the spring of 1943. Here, a PzKpfw IV Ausf G of 20. Panzer-Division is shown in the foreground and two PzKpfw III Ausf M behind during the summer 1943 fighting around Kursk.

This PzKpfw IV Ausf H of 6./SS-PzRgt 12 (12. SS-Panzer-Division *Hitlerjugend*) is shown after its capture by the British during Operation *Epsom* in late June 1944. The white stars were added after its capture. This tank was sent back to Britain and served as the basis for Allied intelligence reports on the PzKpfw IV Ausf H.

existing PzKpfw III and PzKpfw IV tanks. Several guns were considered for up-arming the PzKpfw IV. Some thought had been given to the use of the 5cm L/60 gun as early as May 1941 and Krupp was authorized to build a prototype. However, the Heer was not entirely happy with this option since the PzKpfw IV had always been intended to provide high-explosive firepower; the 5cm guns did not have an especially effective high-explosive round. The alternative was the new 7.5cm KwK 40 L/43 gun. This was a more versatile gun that offered excellent antitank performance as well as high-explosive firepower. Due to the urgency of the situation, this gun began to be mounted on the existing PzKpfw IV Ausf F in March 1942, originally designated as PzKpfw IV Ausf F2. When deployed by the Deutsches Afrikakorps, it was nicknamed the PzKpfw IV *Spezial*, which was adapted by British intelligence as the "Mark IV Special." In the Heer, the short and long versions were usually dubbed *kurz* and *lang*. This version of the PzKpfw IV with the L/43 gun was subsequently designated as the PzKpfw IV Ausf G. These were produced from May 1942 to June 1943. Aside from the gun improvement, there were also additional improvements to the armor during the course of the production run.

An important consequence of the gun programs in early 1942 was that it shifted the focus of German tank production from the PzKpfw III to the PzKpfw IV. The narrow hull superstructure of the PzKpfw III limited the size of the turret ring, thereby limiting the power of gun that could be mounted in the turret. Although the PzKpfw III could be fitted with the 5cm L/60 gun or the short 7.5cm L/24 gun, its turret ring could not withstand the recoil energy of the 7.5cm L/42 gun. As a result,

PzKpfw IV Ausf H, 5./PzLehrRgt 130, JULY 1944

Crew	5
Length	5.92m
Width (without skirts)	2.84m
Height	2.68m
Combat weight	26 metric tonnes
Main gun	7.5cm KwK 40 L/48, 85 rounds
Elevation	−8 to +20 degrees
Machine guns	One coaxial MG 34, one hull-mounted MG 34
Radio	FuG 5 transceiver
Engine	Maybach HL 120 TRM, 195kW (265hp)
Fuel capacity	470 liters
Range	210km
Top speed	38km/h
Armor	50mm gun mantlet, 80mm hull front, 30mm side, 30mm turret rear

5.92m

2.68m

2.84m

A PzKpfw IV Ausf H, tactical number 802, of Oberleutnant Wilhelm Tulzer, of 8./PzRgt 3 (2. Panzer-Division), knocked out during the fighting in Pont-Farcy on August 2, 1944, while trying to stem the *Cobra* breakout. This particular tank, serial 89435, was built at the Nibelungenwerk in April 1944.

the PzKpfw III was no longer suitable as the principal tank of the Panzer divisions due to its firepower limitations. The PzKpfw IV, originally conceived as support tank for the PzKpfw III, now became the principal battle tank of the Panzer divisions.

There were many improvements introduced into the PzKpfw IV Ausf G during the course of its production. From the standpoint of firepower, this included the adoption of a longer L/48 version of the 7.5cm KwK 40 in April 1943. This gun had already been adopted on the StuG III assault gun in July 1942. The thin side armor of the PzKpfw IV left it vulnerable to the ubiquitous Soviet 14.5mm antitank rifles. In April 1943, the PzKpfw IV Ausf G began to be fitted with 5–9mm turret and hull skirts (*Schürzen*).

The next stage of evolution of the PzKpfw IV was the Ausf H. This was essentially the same as the late-production Ausf G except for a series of small changes including a new planetary drive cover and thicker turret-roof armor. It was armed with the new 7.5cm KwK 40 L/48 gun and incorporated all of the other improvements of the late Ausf G. Production began in April 1943 and continued through July 1944. As a result, most of the PzKpfw IV that saw combat in France in the summer of 1944 were this version. The PzKpfw IV Ausf H first began to be deployed in May 1943 as part of the usual cycle of building up Panzer units prior to the summer campaign season in the Soviet Union.

Although the PzKpfw IV had been markedly inferior to the new T-34 in the summer of 1941, by 1942–43 it had become clearly superior in most respects. The L/48 gun had better performance than the Soviet 76mm gun, and PzKpfw IV armor had markedly improved. A later Soviet assessment of comparative technical characteristics of tank in 1943–44 favored the PzKpfw IV over the T-34. The PzKpfw III was assigned a value of 1.00; the T-34/76 scored 1.16; the PzKpfw IV, 1.27; the T-34-85, 1.32; and the Panther, 2.37.

The PzKpfw IV Ausf H began to be replaced on the assembly lines in February 1944 by the Ausf J. This dropped the auxiliary turret-traverse generator motor in favor of additional fuel stowage. Turret traverse at this point was manual, using a new two-speed hand-crank supplemented with an auxiliary crank in the loader's station. The PzKpfw IV manufactured at the Nibelungenwerk from February to May 1944 under Ausf H contracts had the turret-rotation changes implemented before delivery. Most of the Panzer regiments discussed in this book had already been equipped with the Ausf H, but a few Ausf J were received later.

M4 MEDIUM TANK

US medium tank development in the interwar years was hampered by a lack of funding. Production of the M2 medium tank did not begin until the summer of 1939, followed by the production of the modestly improved M2A1 in December 1940. This tank was armed with a 37mm gun and multiple machine guns, and it was already obsolete when it entered service due to poor armor and an archaic layout.

The French government had dispatched manufacturing plans for the Char B1 bis battle tank and Somua S 35 cavalry tank to the United States in 1940 in hopes of starting manufacture in the United States. The defeat of France in June 1940 put an end to this effort. However, Ordnance engineers had the opportunity to examine the Char B1 bis design and this served as the inspiration for the next iteration of the American medium tank, the M3. As in the case of the Char B1 bis, the main 75mm gun was mounted in the hull on the right side, while a 37mm gun was mounted in a small turret on the left side of the superstructure roof. Production started in June 1941 and was bolstered by large export orders to Britain. Although the M3 was a significant improvement in firepower and armor over the M2A1 medium tank, the Armored Force was extremely unhappy with the layout and wanted a more conventional design with the 75mm gun mounted in a turret.

The new medium tank design with the turret-mounted 75mm gun began in February 1941 under the experimental designation of T6. It used the chassis and power-train of the M3 medium tank, but it had a new cast turret and hull. The design

The T6 medium tank pilot differed from the M4A1 production version in many details including the hull side doors, side turret port, and gunner's periscopic sight. The pilot was armed with the short M2 75mm gun while the production series switched to the longer M3 75mm gun.

was also influenced by British requirements since the British Army planned to order a significant number of these tanks through Lend Lease. The T6 was accepted for service as the M4 medium tank in February 1942. To expedite production, two different hull configurations were developed using welded armor plate or a single piece casting. The welded-hull version was designated as the M4 while the cast-hull version was designated as the M4A1; these types were otherwise identical. The M4A1 started production first in February 1942 at the Lima Locomotive plant, and M4 production started in July 1942 at the Pressed Steel Car plant. The US Army had planned to equip both the 1st and 2nd Armored divisions with the M4A1 in the summer of 1942. In the event, the M4A1 tanks intended for the 1st Armored Division were diverted to the British Army in North Africa after the fall of Tobruk due to an urgent requirement. The British Army named the M4 medium tank the General Sherman after the Civil War commander. The Sherman was more popular than the earlier M3 Lee/Grant medium tanks due to the more practical turret.

El Alamein witnessed the first encounters between the Sherman and the PzKpfw IV Ausf G. A British report immediately after El Alamein summarized the initial reactions. "First reports from the Western Desert indicate great satisfaction with Sherman. Position of gun has enabled maximum concealment in hull down position combined with good observation by commander. Have definite evidence of enemy tanks including Mark IV Special being destroyed at ranges up to two thousand yards." The M4 saw its combat debut in US Army service during Operation *Torch* in North Africa in November 1942. The first encounters between US Army M4 and M4A1 Shermans and the PzKpfw IV *lang* took place in Tunisia in February 1943. There were subsequent combat encounters on Sicily in July 1943, and on the Italian mainland starting with the Salerno landings in September 1943. Although US tankers in Italy thought that the 7.5cm gun on the PzKpfw IV was superior to that on the Sherman, there was no particular concern about confronting this tank since its turret-front and side armor were vulnerable at normal combat ranges. Italy was not well suited to maneuver battles, and the Sherman was used primarily in the infantry-support role.

Not all Shermans received the full "Quick Fix" package prior to their commitment to Normandy. This M4 of B/747th Tank Battalion has the added armor appliqué but is still fitted with the M34 gun mount that lacked the telescopic sight. It was knocked out on June 20, 1944, by a German antitank rocket during fighting near Villiers-Fossard in support of the 29th Infantry Division against 353. Infanterie-Division.

Improvements to the M4 and M4A1 were undertaken in response to battle experience by both British and American tank crews. The British Army pressed for the substitution of a coaxial telescopic gun sight in place of the original periscopic sight. British experience suggested that the periscopic sight was too vulnerable to being knocked out of alignment. This change was approved on October 1, 1942, and incorporated into the M34A1 combination gun mount which modified the entire gun mantlet to accommodate the new telescopic sight; production began in March–April 1943. The British also felt that the ammunition racks in the hull sponsons were too

M4A1 MEDIUM TANK, E/66TH ARMORED, JULY 1944

Crew	5
Length	19.2ft (5.9m)
Width	8.6ft (2.6m)
Height	8.7ft (2.7m)
Combat weight	33.4 US tons (30.3 metric tonnes)
Main gun	M3 75mm L/38 gun, 90 rounds
Elevation	−12 to +25 degrees
Machine guns	Two .30-caliber, one .50-caliber
Radio	SCR-508
Engine	Continental R975-C1, 350hp
Fuel capacity	175 US gallons (662 liters)
Range	120 miles (193km)
Top speed	24mph (39km/h)
Armor	76mm gun mantlet, 51mm hull front, 38mm side, 51mm turret rear

5.9m

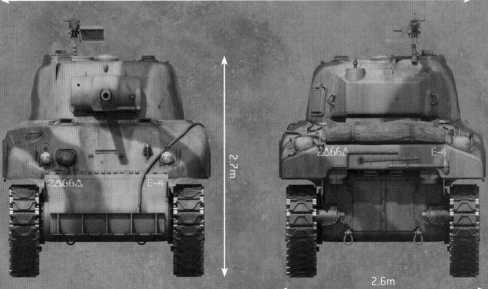

2.7m

2.6m

COMPLETE ROUND, PROJECTILE, A.P.C., 75 mm, M61

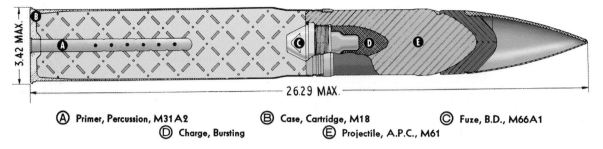

3.42 MAX.

26.29 MAX.

Ⓐ Primer, Percussion, M31A2   Ⓑ Case, Cartridge, M18   Ⓒ Fuze, B.D., M66A1
Ⓓ Charge, Bursting   Ⓔ Projectile, A.P.C., M61

The 75mm M61 used by the M4A1 tank was typical of the armor-piercing-capped-ballistic-cap (APCBC) projectiles of this period. The projectile (E) consisted of three metal sections: the main steel projectile body surmounted by a soft iron cap, and finally a thin sheet-metal ballistic shield in the front. The burster charge (D) at the base of the projectile exploded after penetration to enhance the damage inside the tank.

vulnerable and the principal cause for catastrophic tank fires, accounting for 90 percent of the tank fires. As a short-term solution, a program was approved on November 12, 1942, to begin adding appliqué armor on the hull sides over the ammunition racks. This was also extended to the right front of the turret since anomalies in the turret casting left this section weak. The bulges over the driver/co-driver positions were also fitted with an additional 1¾in (44mm) plate on the welded-hull tanks.

Another method to reduce the probability of tank fires was to reposition the ammunition from the sponsons down into the floor of the hull and to encase the ammunition racks with an outer shell that could be filled with water or other fluids. This "wet" stowage was intended to reduce the probability of the ammunition being ignited by hot shrapnel or embers if the tank was penetrated. This required the turret basket to be completely re-designed, so it was not approved until February 6, 1943. Due to the delay, the first 75mm Sherman tanks with "wet" stowage did not appear in France in any significant numbers until the late summer of 1944. Since many of the original US Army tank units had M4 and M4A1 tanks that had been manufactured in 1942 prior to the improvements, a "Quick Fix" program was implemented in Britain in 1943 to bring the early Sherman tanks up to current standards in terms of important changes such as the M34A1 gun mount and appliqué armor. These were manufactured as "Blitz kits" in the US and shipped to Britain to be incorporated into the tanks at local depots. Most, but not all, tanks in the ETO had these upgrades by the time of the D-Day landings in June 1944.

In late 1943, the Army Service Forces dispatched a "New Weapons Board" to the Mediterranean Theater of Operations (MTO) and European Theater of Operations (ETO) with the dual mission of collecting information on the performance of existing US Army weapons as well as informing units deployed overseas of planned improvements in weapons. Their report, published in April 1944, provides some insight into the general attitude within the US Army to the performance of the M4 and M4A1 tanks prior to the Normandy campaign. Overall, the report concluded that "The medium tanks of the M4 series are well liked by the using personnel … The M4 tank is good and well liked by everyone. However, the fact that the M4 is the outstanding tank of the war to date should not deter us from giving them a better one." In terms of firepower, troops in the MTO felt that the German 7.5cm gun offered better performance than the Sherman's 75mm gun and "there is overwhelming demand for 76mm guns in M4 tanks."

An M4 named *Fury* of F/66th Armored at the start of Operation *Cobra* with an infantry team from the 22nd Infantry Regiment (4th Division) on board.

"Opinion of proper armor thickness was divided. Armored Force troops generally regard the present armor as adequate. They do not want to sacrifice maneuverability, speed, or floatation to gain additional armor protection." Troops were not overly concerned about the hazards of ammunition stowage: "There is no interest in further protection of ammunition if it would entail any decrease in the number of rounds carried. Ready racks in the turret are particularly desired and the tank crews are extremely reluctant to give up ready racks even to increase safety … Tank crews are very little concerned with protection of ammunition and consider accessibility and quantity of primary importance." Tank gunners were not especially happy about the new M55 telescopic gun sights. They found that misalignment was more troublesome than the older M4 periscopic sights and that it offered unsatisfactory light-transmission characteristics, making sighting difficult. Furthermore, many tank crews tended to add a steel helmet over the tanker helmet, making it difficult for the gunner to get their heads in a proper position to use the telescopic sight. Troops in the Italian theater were especially concerned about track improvements since travel on poor mountain roads and hilly terrain led to track throwing.

The US Army began examining more powerful guns for the Sherman in 1942. The ultimate solution was the M1 76mm gun that began to be incorporated into the new M4A1 (76mm) tank starting with January 1944 production. The story of this variant is largely outside the scope of this book, but is told in greater detail elsewhere.[2] It has some bearing on this particular study since the 2nd and 3rd Armored divisions were the first units to receive these up-armed tanks prior to Operation *Cobra*.

2 Steven Zaloga, *M4 (76mm) Sherman Medium Tank 1943–65* (Osprey New Vanguard 73: 2003).

TECHNICAL SPECIFICATIONS

PROTECTION

Although the Sherman is often maligned for its poor armor protection, it was better protected than the PzKpfw IV Ausf H from nearly all aspects. Nevertheless, the Sherman's armor was not sufficient to protect it from frontal attack by the PzKpfw IV at typical battle ranges due to the excellent performance of the 7.5cm KwK 40 gun. The Sherman's gun was adequate to defeat the turret armor of the PzKpfw IV Ausf H at normal combat ranges, but not the front of the superstructure. Both tanks were capable of defeating one another in side attacks. The data presented here is provided both with actual thickness and angle, as well as equivalent thickness. An armor plate angled at 30 degrees offers about 15 percent better protection than the same plate at a vertical angle due to geometry; this data does not consider the ricochet factor since the APCBC (armor-piercing, capped, ballistic-cap) ammunition used at this time was less prone to this effect except at extreme angles.

FIREPOWER

The German 7.5cm KwK 40 gun offered superior anti-armor firepower to the American 75mm M3 gun. The superiority of the German gun was due to longer barrel

Comparative armor protection

	PzKpfw IV Ausf H		M4A1	
	Actual thickness	Equivalent thickness	Actual thickness	Equivalent thickness
Hull front superstructure	80mm @ 8°	81mm	51+45mm* @ 35/55°	89+55mm (144mm)
Lower hull front	80mm @14°	82mm	51mm @ 58°	~96mm***
Hull superstructure sides	30mm @ 0°+7mm @ 0°	30mm+7mm (37mm)**	38+25mm* @ 0°	38+25mm (63mm)
Hull upper rear	20mm @ 10°	20mm	38mm @ 10°	39mm
Turret front	50mm @ 5°	50mm	76+20mm* @ 30°	88+23mm (111mm)
Mantlet	50mm @ 15°	52mm	76mm @ ~45°	~107mm***
Turret sides	30mm @ 25° +7mm @ 0°	33mm+7mm (40mm)**	51mm @ 5°	51mm
Turret rear	30mm @ 18°	32mm	51mm @ 8°	51mm

*Appliqué armor.   **When fitted with Schürzen.   ***Rounded surface.

length as well as a greater propellant charge. Both factors contributed in providing about 25 percent better muzzle velocity and impact energy. The American 75mm M3 gun was adequate when dealing with the earlier versions of the PzKpfw IV, but it slipped once the Wehrmacht began increasing the frontal armor of its tanks.

Both tank guns relied primarily on APCBC ammunition. Tank ammunition during World War II evolved from AP (armor-piercing) solid shot to APC (armor-piercing capped) to deal with the tendency of the streamlined AP shot to ricochet off angled plate or shatter against face-hardened plate. Capped ammunition consisted of a blunt,

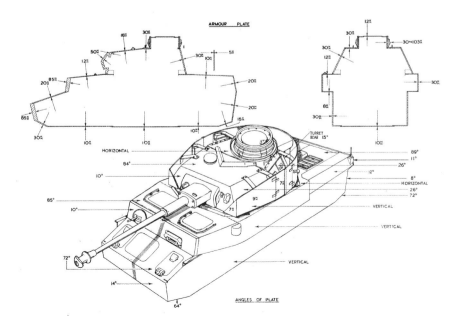

This Allied illustration shows the armor thickness and angles of the PzKpfw IV Ausf H. It was based on a captured example from 12. SS-Panzer-Division *Hitlerjugend*, tactical number 635, serial number 86934, built at the Nibelungenwerk in October 1943. It is typical of PzKpfw IV tanks in Normandy, except for the V-shaped armor strip added in front of the commander's cupola, presumably a *Hitlerjugend* improvisation.

The Sherman's armor was not adequate when facing the newer German weapons including the 7.5cm PaK 40 and the Panther's 7.5cm KwK 42. This particular M4A1 is engaged in an unequal duel with a Panther from Panzer-Lehr-Division, and is shown here on July 20 after the German panzer offensive on the Vire River had been beaten back. Besides the six hits from the Panther's 7.5cm gun there are two smaller holes on the M4A1 from *Panzerfaust* or *Panzerschreck* antitank weapons.

soft-metal cap at the front of the projectile that was less prone to the problem of ricochet or projectile break-up than hardened steel. True APC ammunition was short-lived since the blunt front end degraded the velocity of the projectile. Instead, APC ammunition quickly evolved into APCBC (APC with ballistic cap) that added a thin metal ballistic windshield to improve the ballistics of the projectile. It is worth noting that the US Army referred to its armor-piercing ammunition as APC when it was in fact APCBC.

The Wehrmacht adopted HVAP (high-velocity armor-piercing) ammunition late in 1941 in response to the thicker armor on the Soviet T-34 and KV tanks. HVAP was a lightweight projectile based around a dense sub-caliber tungsten-carbide core within a light metal body, typically aluminum. This offered superior muzzle velocity and penetration at shorter ranges. However, tungsten carbide was a scarce resource in Germany and so the 7.5cm PzGr 40 round was seldom if ever issued to PzKpfw IV units in France in 1944. The Wehrmacht also developed a shaped-charge projectile (HEAT: high explosive antitank) for the short 7.5cm L/24 gun, but this seldom was used with the L/48 gun since the fusing was not adequate to cope with the high velocity of this gun. The US Army was slow to adopt HVAP ammunition for tanks. By the time it was issued, starting in August 1944, priority went to tanks with the 76mm gun and tank destroyers with the 3in gun. The US Army also developed a

A view from the loader's side showing the mounting for the 7.5cm KwK 40. This is inside PzKpfw IV Ausf G chassis number 83072, captured by the British Army during the North African campaign.

75mm shaped-charge antitank projectile, but as in the German case, it was limited to use from low-velocity howitzers. HEAT ammunition did not become common for tank ammunition until the late 1940s when the development of piezo-electric fuzes permitted ignition of the warhead quickly enough for the shaped charge to function properly.

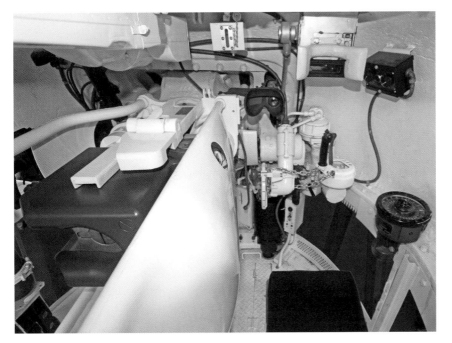

A view inside a Sherman turret from the tank commander's station with the gunner's seat and fire controls immediately in front and the 75mm gun breech to the left. The Sherman gunner had the option of using either the coaxial telescopic sight to the left or the periscopic telescopic sight to the upper right for aiming the gun.

COMPARATIVE FIREPOWER

The table below compares the parameters of the two tank guns. It should be noted that performance data is based on averages. The penetration figures cited below are based on official German and American documents yet give different penetration values. This is due to the fact that penetration varied depending on the type of armor being struck. For example, in the case of the US 75mm M61 projectile, the stated performance at 500yd was 2.9in (74mm) against homogenous rolled armor plate, but 3.4in (86mm) against face-hardened armor plate. In addition, initial muzzle velocity and therefore penetration also depended on ambient air temperature and the specifics of the propellant which varied during production.

	PzKpfw IV Ausf H	M4A1
Gun	7.5cm KwK 40	75mm M3
Bore	75mm	75mm
Length (calibers)	L/48	L/38
Stowed main gun ammunition	85	90
Armor-piercing round	PzGr 39 (**1**)	M61 (**3**)
Casing	6339 St.	M18, M18B1
Muzzle velocity (m/sec)	704–790	620–625
Round weight (kg)	11.5	9.0
Projectile weight (kg)	6.9	6.8
Propellant weight (kg)	2.4	0.98
Penetration in mm @ 500m @ 30°	91–96	62–67
High-explosive round	SprGr 34 (**2**)	M48 (**4**)
Round weight (kg)	8.7	8.5
Projectile weight (kg)	5.69	6.7
High-explosive weight (grams)	653	667

1

2

3

4

14 Jg.2.42N

III

Jg 9.242 N

75 G
U.APC-TM61

75 G
TNT
SHELL M48
+

7,5 cm Stu.K.40

7,5 cm Kw.K.40

2,43 kg

RP-61-(420/590-3.8/1.5)

dbg 1942/5

Jg 9.2.42 N

7,5 cm Stu.K.40

7,5 cm Kw.K.40

755 g

BL.P.-A0-(4.4-0.6)

dbg 1942/5

Jg 9.2.42 N

Although most accounts of tank guns focus on their antitank performance, high-explosive ammunition was used far more widely. US Army 75mm tank ammunition expenditure in the ETO was 71 percent high-explosive, 19 percent armor-piercing, and 10 percent smoke. Both the 7.5cm KwK 40 and 75mm M3 guns had similar high-explosive throwing power. Both guns could also use smoke projectiles. The German NbgrPatr smoke projectile was a conventional type using an oleum/pumice fill and base ejection. The US 75mm M64 was a newer type of smoke projectile, actually classified as a chemical round, since it used WP (white phosphorus) as its filler. Aside from proving useful for creating obscuring smoke clouds, the WP round had a useful secondary feature as an incendiary round. One of the novel applications for the "Willy Pete" round was in tank fighting. After encounters with the Panther tank in Normandy, US tank crews quickly learned that it was invulnerable to frontal attack using APC ammunition. However, it was discovered that a "Willy Pete" round fired against the front of the Panther would blind the enemy tank and make it possible for the Sherman unit to maneuver to attack its weaker side armor. A secondary effect was that the turret ventilators in German tanks would suck in the noxious fumes from the white phosphorus, sometimes forcing German crews to abandon their tanks. Some US tank crewmen interviewed by the author said that they often used "Willy Pete" against German tanks, especially in the later months of the war, as inexperienced German tankers after being hit with smoke would think that their tank was on fire and would abandon it. By mid-June 1944, the use of "Willy Pete" in tank fighting was disseminated widely in US tank units in Normandy as a useful tactic and became SOP (standard operating procedure) in some units.

MOBILITY

The mobility of both the M4 Sherman and PzKpfw IV Ausf H were fairly similar. The Sherman had a more powerful engine, but it was also heavier. In the Italian theater, many German tankers considered the Sherman superior in mobility to the German tanks when employed in the mountainous country. The Finnish Army called the PzKpfw IV Ausf J a "shaker" for its rough ride compared to their StuG III which had the torsion-bar suspension of the PzKpfw III. They considered the PzKpfw IV suspension poor, and the bogie mountings as weak and prone to shearing off in rough terrain. The vertical volute suspension on the Sherman offered more road-wheel travel and smoother operation in rough terrain.

Tank-mobility problems in Lower Normandy around Saint-Lô were due to the prevalence of hedgerows, known in French as *bocage*. French farmers had built up these earth-and-foliage barriers over the centuries as a means to protect their pastures from the harsh maritime winds. US Army accounts referred to the bocage as "an inverted trench system" since it created a natural fortification network for defense. Tanks could usually drive over and through the bocage, but to do so made the tank vulnerable since it tended to expose the thin belly armor to the enemy. The US Army began tactical experiments to overcome the mobility restrictions of the bocage in July 1944 using improvised hedge cutters. The first of these, dubbed the "Salad Fork," was tested during an attack near Saint-Lô on July 11, 1944, by the 747th Tank Battalion. Two pointed wooden stakes attached to the front of the Sherman would punch holes in the base of the bocage, and accompanying engineers would plant explosive charges in the holes, blowing a gap. This was too time-consuming and expensive. The Salad Fork was followed by the "Green Cutter" used by the 709th and 747th Tank battalions, which was a steel beam welded to the front of the tank to plow through the bocage. A better hedge-buster was subsequently developed by Sgt Curtis Culin using

A composite-hull M4 of the 3rd Armored Division is shown passing by an abandoned 8.8cm Flak gun in August 1944. During Operation *Cobra*, the M4 tanks of the 3rd Armored Division were fitted with a different type of Rhino hedgerow cutter called a "Richardson Device" which differed from the Culin type in the triangular design of its outer cutting prongs.

steel prongs; this was dubbed the "Rhino." A variation on this using larger triangular prongs was used by the 3rd Armored Division and other units as the "Richardson Device." Local production of the hedge cutters was undertaken by First US Army ordnance units to equip several hundred tanks prior to Operation *Cobra*. Besides the Rhino devices, M4 tanks fitted with the M1 dozer blade proved very versatile during Operation *Cobra*, and besides being used to cut openings in the bocage, they were also widely used as route-clearance vehicles to push abandoned heavy vehicles off major roads. The Wehrmacht was not especially innovative in the use of combat-engineer armored vehicles, and lacked armored dozers, mine clearing vehicles, or improvised hedge-busters.

Comparative mobility data		
	PzKpfw IV Ausf H	M4A1
Engine type	Maybach HL 120 TRM inline V12	Continental R975 C1, 9-cylinder radial
Power	195kW	350hp (261kW)
Transmission	Zahnradfabrik SSG 76 Aphon	Caterpillar Synchromesh
Transmission speeds (forward/reverse)	6/1	5/1
Steering	Krupp/Wilson clutch steering	Controlled differential
Power-to-weight ratio	7.5kW/tonne	10.5hp/T (8.61kW/tonne)
Maximum road speed	38km/h	24mph (38km/h)
Tank loaded weight	26.0 metric tonnes	33.4 US tons (30.3 metric tonnes)
Fuel	470 liters; gasoline	175 US gallons (662 liters); gasoline
Maximum range	210km	193km
Ground pressure	0.89kg/cm^2	0.96kg/cm^2

THE COMBATANTS

THE CREW

PzKpfw IV Ausf H

The PzKpfw IV crew consisted of five men: three in the turret and two in the hull. The PzKpfw IV had a turret basket with rotating floor. The tank commander (*Kommandant*) sat on "the throne" in the rear center of the turret behind the main

PzKpfw IV Ausf H crew layout.

PzKpfw IV TURRET

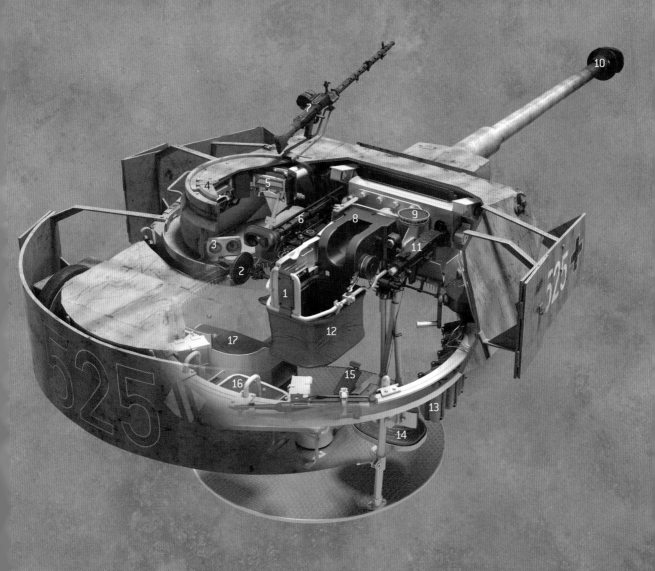

1. Gun guard
2. Gunner's gun-elevation wheel
3. Gunner's azimuth indicator
4. Commander's cupola
5. Commander's vision device
6. Gunner's TZF 5b telescopic sight

7. MG 34 machine gun
8. 7.5cm KwK 40 gun breech
9. Turret ventilation fan
10. Muzzle brake
11. Coaxial MG 34 machine gun
12. Shell-casing catch bag

13. Spare 7.62mm ammunition bags
14. Loader's seat
15. Gunner's foot trigger
16. Commander's seat
17. Gunner's seat

The radio in the PzKpfw IV was located in the right hull front and operated by the *Funker* (radioman). He was also responsible for the hull machine gun. The crew communicated using an internal intercom system including throat microphones, as is evident from the headphones and wiring.

gun. Above the throne was an armored cupola with vision ports that were shielded externally by armored visors and 50mm-thick bullet-resistant glass. In addition, the cupola had an overhead hatch that allowed the commander to operate with his head out of the tank for better situational awareness. The commander communicated with the crew via a throat microphone and intercom system.

The gunner (*Richtkanonier*) was located in the left side of the turret. The main gun was aimed using a TZF 5b telescopic sight. The gunner could traverse the turret either with a mechanical hand-wheel or an electric drive powered off an auxiliary motor that could turn the turret 360 degrees in 23 seconds. A British report concluded that "the maximum speed (of the electric traverse) is relatively low, but the response is quick and the braking good ... The number of resistance steps is too small with the result that the characteristic is noticeably stepped, making it impossible to follow moving targets accurately particularly at low angular speeds." The hand-gear required 190 turns for a complete rotation of the turret.

The loader (*Ladekanonier*) had a seat on the right side of the turret but in action the seat would be folded and the loader would stand on the turret basket floor. The ammunition was distributed around the PzKpfw IV's interior in several bins scattered around the fighting compartment; those in the driver's compartment were accessed with the assistance of the radio operator. The loader was also responsible for loading the coaxial machine gun which was directly in front of him.

The driver (*Fahrer*) was located in the left front of the

The *Fahrer* (driver) sat in the left hull front. His seat could be elevated when traveling outside the combat zone for better vision. He has a headset and throat microphone for communicating with the rest of the crew. This is an *Oberfeldwebel* of PzBrig 111 in Lorraine in September 1944.

hull. Steering was a conventional Wilson clutch-steering type manufactured by Krupp with the transmission in the front center of the hull and the steering brakes forward of the driver. The driver had a direct-vision port with armored cover immediately in front of him protected by thick glass; he lacked the binocular telescope found in earlier versions of the PzKpfw IV.

The radio operator (*Funker*) sat in the right front hull opposite the driver. The FuG 5 radio transmitter–receiver was mounted centrally above the transmission to the left of the radio-operator. This was a voice/telegraphic AM radio with two preset channels and an effective range of about 2km in voice mode. It suffered from the inherent shortcomings of AM radios in tanks, namely the susceptibility to static noise which made the set useless during travel. It was also less powerful than US tank radios, with only 10 watts of forward power versus 30 watts.

M4A1

The crew of the M4A1 was five men and their roles were similar to those in the PzKpfw IV. The turret layout between the PzKpfw IV and Sherman was inverted with the Sherman gunner on the right side of the turret and the loader on the left. The tank commander sat immediately behind the gunner. The commander sat under a traversable cupola with a periscope fitted to one of the two hatch halves. This offered poorer situational awareness than the commander's cupola on the PzKpfw IV. A new all-vision cupola for the Sherman was already in production but it did not reach service in France in significant numbers except on the M4A1 (76mm) and the new "wet stowage" Shermans. As in the German case, US tank commanders were encouraged to operate outside the cupola for better situational awareness in combat. Unlike the German layout, the commander was responsible for operating the tank

LEFT A sergeant of the 66th Armored Regiment (2nd Armored Division) fits a periscope into the driver's hatch of an M4A1 medium tank on July 24, 1944, the day before the start of Operation *Cobra*. This provides a good view of the standard Rawlings helmet issued to US tank crews, based on a prewar football helmet.

RIGHT The crew members of an M4A1 of the 66th Armored Regiment (2nd Armored Division) load 75mm ammunition into their tank on July 24, 1944. This particular tank, from the May 1943 production batch, has the sealed pistol port on the turret. This feature was later reinstated as it was a more convenient way to load ammunition.

radio that was located in the rear bustle; the loader was cross-trained to assist the commander with the radio. The US Army was the first to adopt FM radios for tanks which reduced the radios' vulnerability to noise static and it was a generation more advanced than the German tank radios of the period. The Sherman crew had an intercom system for internal communication.

The gunner could aim the 75mm gun using either an M55 coaxial telescopic sight or an M4 telescopic sight within the M4 periscope. The periscopic sight offered the Sherman gunner better situational awareness than his German counterpart and reduced the initial time of firing. The gunner traversed the turret using hydraulic power traverse which was faster than the PzKpfw IV's electric traverse, 15 seconds versus 23 seconds for a full 360-degree traverse.

The loader had a folding seat on the left side of the turret. The ammunition layout on the Sherman varied through time. The early-production Shermans had ready rounds stowed along the walls of the turret basket. This limited access to the sponson bins, and units began to cut away the walls. A reconfiguration of the turret basket was approved on June 4, 1943, and led to production changes as well. US tank crews typically carried as much ammunition as possible, often loading an additional 30 rounds or more on the turret floor.

In the hull, the driver sat on the left side and the co-driver/bow machine-gunner sat on the right. Although the early-production M4 and M4A1 had a direct-vision port in front of both stations, this was eliminated when appliqué armor was mounted. The primary means of vision when in combat was through traversable periscopes in the hatches. The .30-caliber bow machine gun was intended mainly for suppressive fire. There was no dedicated sight as was fitted on the German hull machine guns.

M4A1 TURRET

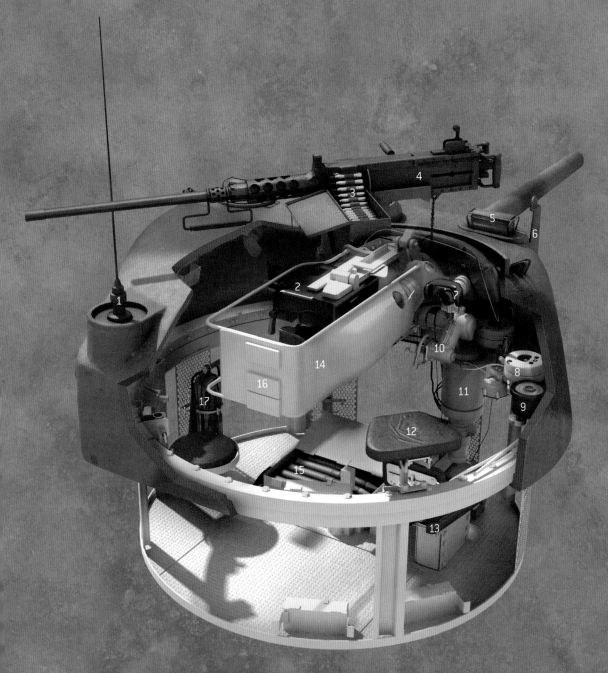

1. Radio antenna
2. 75mm gun breech
3. .50-caliber ammunition box
4. M2HB .50-caliber heavy machine gun
5. Gunner's periscopic sight
6. Blade sight
7. Gunner's M55 telescopic sight
8. Turret-traverse control
9. Gunner's azimuth indicator
10. Gunner's gun elevation wheel
11. Hydraulic turret-traverse mechanism
12. Commander's seat
13. Gunner's seat
14. Gun guard
15. Floor 75mm ready ammunition rack
16. Gun counterweights
17. Fire extinguisher

TRAINING

PANZER-LEHR-DIVISION

The unit most directly in the path of Operation *Cobra* was Panzer-Lehr-Division, commanded by Generalleutnant Fritz Bayerlein, Rommel's executive officer during the North African campaign. Panzer-Lehr-Division was one of the last Heer Panzer divisions to be formed. It was specifically intended to fight against the expected Allied invasion of France. Panzer-Lehr-Division was built around training and demonstration units, including Panzertruppenschule II Krampnitz near Berlin, hence the *Lehr* (training/demonstration) name. The division's troops were a mixture of combat veterans from the training units combined with new recruits. In April 1944, the division was designated as 130. Panzer-Lehr-Division, though it was usually called simply Panzer-Lehr-Division. The division organized and trained in Lorraine in the Verdun–Nancy area of France, but was hurriedly dispatched to Hungary in the spring of 1944 as part of Operation *Margarethe* due to the crisis on that front. It returned to France and by early June it was in the Le Mans area, within range of Normandy. It was the best-equipped and -trained Panzer unit in Normandy.

Panzer-Lehr-Division was based around a single Panzer regiment and two *Panzergrenadier* regiments. Panzer-Lehr-Regiment, also known as PzLehrRgt 130, had the standard organization of one battalion of Panthers and one battalion of PzKpfw IV. It was commanded by Oberst Rudolf Gerhardt, an experienced tank commander. He led II./PzRgt 7 in the Soviet Union during 1941 and later served in the Tunisian campaign. The division's I. Abteilung was in fact the Panther-equipped I./PzRgt 6 which did not return from the Eastern Front until June 10, 1944.

The division's PzKpfw IV battalion, II./PzLehrRgt 130, was built around a *Lehrtruppe* stationed previously with the Panzertruppenschule in Bergen/Fallingbostel. It was commanded by Major Prinz Wilhelm von Schönburg-Waldenburg. The prince had led a company of PzRgt 31 and received the Iron Cross for his leadership during the Battle of France in 1940. He was killed in action during the battalion's combat debut on June 11, 1944, when his command tank was hit by a British 6-pdr antitank gun during the fighting at Point 103 west of Cristot. The battalion's tanks carried a white rhomboid with two red lines, a simplified version of the Prince's family coat of arms. One of the company commanders, Hauptmann Helmut Ritgen, took over command. Ritgen later recalled about the unit that:

the officer cadre was first-rate. So was my Panzer company. The battalion exuded discipline and confidence …

Starting in mid-March 1944, Panzer-Lehr-Division took part in Operation *Margarethe*, the German occupation of Hungary. Here, a column of infantry half-tracks of PzGrLehrRgt 901 parades down Erzsébet Boulevard in central Budapest as a show of force. The two lead vehicles are SdKfz 251/3 Ausf C radio command vehicles.

During the *Cobra* battles, 7./PzLehrRgt 130 would be commanded by Leutnant Freiherr von Landsberg-Velen, pictured here in the cupola of his PzKpfw IV Ausf H when he led 2. Zug of the company under Ritgen's command during Operation *Margarethe* in Hungary during April 1944. (Helmut Ritgen)

the officers and NCOs were well trained "old hands," most had front line experience and they had faith in the regiment and its weapons. Certainly we would have preferred Panthers in place of our PzKpfw IVs, but we still had faith and pride in them.

The battalion received its shipment of 98 PzKpfw IV Ausf H tanks in February 1944, and had a few older tanks from its original Bergen deployment. Besides the headquarters, the battalion had four tank companies numbered 5. to 8. with 22 PzKpfw IV in each company. I./PzRgt 6 had a strength of 89 Panther tanks on D-Day. Other major AFVs in the division included 41 assault guns and tank destroyers with PzJgLehrAbt 130, which had one company of the new Jagdpanzer IV and two companies of StuG III assault guns. The division was exceptionally well equipped with armored infantry and reconnaissance vehicles, and was the only division to have its four *Panzergrenadier* battalions entirely equipped with armored half-tracks. There were 693 SdKfz 250 and SdKfz 251 armored half-tracks at the start of the campaign.

This PzKpfw IV Ausf H of II./PzLehrRgt 130 was filmed moving to the front line on June 16, 1944, during the fighting against British units in the Tilly-sur-Seulles sector. German tanks in Normandy were usually camouflaged with foliage as defense against Allied fighter-bomber attack.

In terms of personnel, the division was near full-strength on D-Day. In assessing unit strength, the Heer generally distinguished between authorized strength according to the tables of organization (*Sollstärke*), overall strength (*Kopfstärke*) based on the actual number of troops in the unit at a specific time, and combat strength (*Kampfstärke*) that included only the troops in close-combat units such as Panzer,

Panzergrenadier, Füsilier, Panzerjäger, Panzer-Pionier, etc. At the beginning of June 1944, Panzer-Lehr-Division had an authorized strength of 14,519 officers and men, an actual strength of 13,157 and a combat strength of 7,120 men. It had a number of units attached to it including PzKp 316 (Funklenk) which brought its overall strength up to 14,699 men. The distinction between overall strength and combat strength is important to keep in mind, since a combat loss of 3,500 men would seem to be only about 20 percent of divisional strength when in fact it represented nearly half of combat strength.

Panzer-Lehr-Division was exceptionally well trained since it was formed around the experienced cadres of elite demonstration and training units. The Heer rated the *Kampfwert* (combat value) of its divisions on a scale of 1 to 4, with Kampfwert 1 indicating that the division was suitable for offensive missions; Kampfwert 2 indicating suitability for limited offensive missions; Kampfwert 3 indicating suitability only for defensive missions; and Kampfwert 4 indicating limited suitability for defensive missions. On D-Day, Panzer-Lehr-Division was rated at Kampfwert 1.

The division had a rough introduction into combat on D-Day when it was ordered into the Caen sector on June 7 in broad daylight. It was hit by repeated Allied air strikes, losing five tanks, 85 other armored vehicles and 123 trucks including 80 fuel trucks and 23 prime movers. The division saw extensive combat against British forces in the June battles around Caen, suffering very heavy troop and equipment losses. By June 26, its PzKpfw IV battalion had been reduced from 99 to only 26 operational tanks, with a further 20 in short-term repair, and 20 in long-term repair. The long-term repair category often included tanks wrecked by heavy battle damage and kept on hand for cannibalization. Total losses of PzKpfw IV through July 8 were 36 tanks. The division claimed to have knocked out 85 British tanks and 18 self-propelled guns during the June fighting. Troop casualties in June were 3,407, about half of its combat effectives.

Following the liberation of Cherbourg in late June 1944 by the US Army's VII Corps, the focus of the First US Army attacks shifted south to the Saint-Lô sector. As a result, on July 7, 1944, Panzer-Lehr-Division began to be transferred to the Saint-Jean-de-Daye area as part of the German response. On July 11, four *Kampfgruppen* from the division staged a spoiling attack against US forces over the Vire River near Le Dézert. The attack was a shambles and about half the force was lost. One *Kampfgruppe* including a company of Panther tanks was surrounded and destroyed. II./PzLehrRgt 130 lost eight PzKpfw IV, and two company commanders. For the next two weeks, the battalion was engaged in small-scale skirmishes west of Saint-Lô, attempting to halt the relentless American infantry attacks.

At the time of Operation *Cobra*, LXXXIV. Armeekorps rated Panzer-Lehr-Division at a combat value of 3 due to its battered shape. Of its available six *Panzergrenadier* battalions, three were rated as weak, two as exhausted and one was merely a cadre of the field-replacement battalion. The division's combat strength prior to the start of Operation *Cobra* was only about 2,210 troops plus another 1,000 troops from attached units as detailed below. Tank strength was equally meager with only 12 PzKpfw IV and 16 Panther tanks plus a further 30 in varying states of repair behind the lines. In contrast, the division had good field artillery support with five light and four heavy batteries (16 10.5cm and 12 15cm/15.2cm field howitzers) from its own regiment, plus three heavy batteries (16 15cm howitzers) assigned from 17. SS-Panzergrenadier-Division *Götz von Berlichingen*.

A PzKpfw IV Ausf H of 5./PzLehrRgt 130, one of three knocked out in fighting against M4 tanks of the 743rd Tank Battalion near the hamlet of Le Mesnil-Durand on July 17, 1944. These tanks were supporting PzGrLehrRgt 902 in the defense of a line southwest of Pont-Hébert against the US 30th Infantry Division.

Owing to its weakness in infantry, Panzer-Lehr-Division received a variety of infantry attachments. FJR 14 was detached from 5. Fallschirmjäger-Division and included three battalions rated at strong, average and weak. In spite of their reputation, Bayerlein had a poor impression of the airborne troops since they were "almost useless as nearly all the time they avoided contact" and discipline was so poor that "in the rear area, there were paratroopers rambling everywhere." Its three companies were stationed along the main line of resistance in PzGrLehrRgt 901's sector north of La Chapelle-en-Juger.

Kampfgruppe Heintz, based on GR 984 of 275. Infanterie-Division, was assigned to Panzer-Lehr-Division, minus one battalion. This reduced force, sometimes called Kampfgruppe Huettlinger, was deployed in the northeast corner of PzGrLehrRgt 901's sector near Hébécrevon and was rated as medium strength with about 200 men. Kampfgruppe Brusow from 2. SS-Panzer-Division *Das Reich* had been assigned but it was pulled back on July 24 for rehabilitation near Gavray due to heavy casualties suffered in the mid-July fighting.

THE OTHER PANZER DIVISIONS

Although Panzer-Lehr-Division was the primary focus of the 2nd Armored Division in the opening stages of Operation *Cobra*, two other German mechanized units were eventually encountered. By late July 1944, 2. SS-Panzer-Division *Das Reich* was the strongest division in AOK 7, and was the only one rated Kampfwert 1. Its lineage can be traced back to several earlier Waffen-SS formations, becoming a *Panzergrenadier* division in November 1942, and converting to a Panzer division on October 15, 1943. The division had fought on the Eastern Front through December 1943 when it was ordered back to Prussia for refitting after having suffered heavy losses. A *Kampfgruppe* remained on the Eastern Front through April 1944 when it was transferred back to its new training grounds near Toulouse, France and amalgamated back into its parent division. At the time, the division was in very poor condition due to the influx of about 9,000 untrained recruits and a lack of experienced NCOs, officers, and equipment. In mid-April 1944, the *Kampfgruppe* was rated at a combat value of 3, while the rest of the division was rated off the scale as non-operational. The division received a considerable amount of new equipment in the month before its transfer to Normandy in mid-June and had 79 PzKpfw IV, 78 Panther and 42 StuG III. The road march of the division from southwestern France to Normandy became infamous when its troops conducted several massacres of French civilians, most notoriously in the village of Oradour-sur-Glane, in retribution for a French resistance ambush.

Units of the division took part in the fighting around Caen in late June 1944, losing 37 tanks through July 3. In early July 1944 the division was shifted to the American sector near Saint-Lô. The division saw extensive fighting against the First US Army prior to the start of Operation *Cobra*. *Das Reich* occupied the forward-most sector of the front, the so-called Carentan–Périers Isthmus. Hitler had ordered a major night spoiling attack by the division in the third week of July 1944, but this never transpired for a variety of reasons. Prior to the American offensive, the division's three available *Panzergrenadier* battalions were rated as strong, medium, and average; a fourth battalion returned shortly before *Cobra*. Armored strength in SS-PzRgt 2 in late July was 37 PzKpfw IV including two command tanks and 37 Panther including two command tanks, as well as 25 assault guns. Its field artillery included its own three 10.5cm batteries and three 15cm batteries, plus three more 10.5cm batteries from neighboring infantry divisions. The division's main reserve consisted of two tank companies moved out of the front lines and placed near Hauteville-la-Guichard.

The third mechanized division under SS-Obergruppenführer Paul Hausser's command was 17. SS-Panzergrenadier-Division *Götz von Berlichingen*. This division had begun to organize in October 1943, and by D-Day, it had a total strength of 17,231 men. However, the division was made up mainly of inadequately trained men and was lacking about 40 percent of its officers and NCOs. The division had a poor reputation among the regular Heer commanders due to very weak divisional leadership, a consequence of its late formation date and the steady drain of the threadbare Waffen-SS officer pool to existing divisions on the Eastern Front to replace combat casualties. Its two *Panzergrenadier* regiments were authorized trucks rather than armored half-tracks, and suffered severe shortages when deployed in Normandy. It had an authorized strength of 1,717 trucks, but on June 1, 1944, had only 220. Two of the *Panzergrenadier* battalions substituted bicycles for trucks. The situation gradually improved and there were 676 trucks on hand in early July 1944. A July 23 report put its motorization level at a paltry 30 percent.

The division's SS-PzAbt 17, commanded by SS-Sturmbannführer Ludwig Kepplinger, was equipped in an expedient fashion with assault guns instead of tanks. It started to receive StuG IV in February 1944 and reached its authorized strength of 42 assault guns in April 1944. The StuG IV was based on the PzKpfw IV tank chassis with the same 7.5cm gun, but in a fixed casemate rather than a turret. This battalion was one of the first elements of the division to see combat a week after D-Day, fighting US paratroopers in the Carentan sector. Its operational assault-gun strength fell continually through the month due to heavy fighting: down to 24 on June 15, 18 on

A pair of PzKpfw IV Ausf J of 6./SS-PzRgt 2 that were knocked out while supporting Kampfgruppe *Wisliceny* during the fighting around Saint-Fromond on July 11, 1944. The nearest tank carries the tactical number 622, indicating 6. Kompanie, 2. Zug, second tank.

June 27, and ten on July 21 shortly before the start of Operation *Cobra*. It suffered nine total losses by the beginning of July 1944, the remaining vehicles being sidelined with battle damage or mechanical problems. Owing to its heavy losses in the Cotentin fighting, the division was assessed at the lowest combat value of 4 prior to Operation *Cobra*. Of its eight *Panzergrenadier* battalions, two were rated as weak, five as exhausted, and one was a cadre of the field-replacement battalion. Its heavy field-artillery batteries had been detached to Panzer-Lehr-Division.

An M4A1 named *Derby* of D/33rd Armored (3rd Armored Division) passes a knocked-out PzKpfw IV Ausf H of 6./SS-PzRgt 2 that was supporting Kampfgruppe *Wisliceny* during the fighting around Saint-Fromond on July 11, 1944.

HELMUT RITGEN

Hauptmann Helmut Ritgen commanded II./PzLehrRgt 130, the PzKpfw IV battalion of Panzer-Lehr-Division at the time of Operation *Cobra*. Ritgen was born in Gehrden on April 10, 1916. He was commissioned as a *Leutnant* in 1938 and served as a platoon commander of 7./PzRgt 11 during the 1939 campaign in Poland and the battle of France in May–June 1940, first serving in a PzKpfw 35(t) in Poland and then a PzKpfw IV in France. He saw extensive combat again with 6. Panzer-Division during Operation *Barbarossa* in 1941. Ritgen was promoted to *Hauptmann* in early 1942 and he was reassigned as the regimental adjutant of PzRgt 11 during its rehabilitation in France. The division returned to the Eastern Front in November 1942 and took part in the bitter relief operations on the southern flank of Stalingrad. In March 1943, Ritgen was reassigned as a company commander in PzLehrRgt 130 in Wünsdorf. After the unit was absorbed into the new Panzer-Lehr-Division, he commanded 7./PzLehrRgt 130, equipped with PzKpfw IV tanks.

When the battalion commander, Major Prinz Wilhelm von Schönburg-Waldenburg, was killed on June 11, 1944, Ritgen was placed in temporary command; he was formally appointed battalion commander on June 22. Ritgen led the afternoon counterattack by 15 PzKpfw IV at Villers-Bocage on June 13; this fighting has largely been overshadowed by the actions of Michael Wittmann and the Tiger tanks of SS-sPzAbt 101. By the end of June 1944, the battalion had lost about half its starting strength with fewer than 50 operational tanks. Panzer-Lehr-Division shifted to the American sector on July 8–10. When Operation *Cobra* was launched on July 25, Ritgen's battalion was down to only 12 PzKpfw IV tanks; most of the battalion's original officers were casualties. On July 26, Ritgen's Panzerbefehlswagen IV was knocked out by air attack, but the crew survived. By July 27, the battalion had been reduced to two functional PzKpfw IV tanks that were detached to the regimental headquarters.

After the unit was refitted, Ritgen remained in battalion command for the remainder of the war, being promoted to *Oberst* by war's end. In December 1944, he was awarded the German Cross in Gold for his leadership of the battalion in the Ardennes fighting. During the war, he had been awarded both classes of the Iron Cross, the Tank Destruction Badge, and the Wound Badge in Silver. Immediately after the war he was a civilian supervisor with the British Army of the Rhine. In 1955, he joined the Bundeswehr, serving at the Münster tank school and as commander of Panzerbataillon 194. Helmut Ritgen died on February 7, 2013.

LINDSAY C. HERKNESS, JR.

Lt Col Lindsay Coates Herkness, Jr. commanded the 2nd Battalion, 66th Armored Regiment (2nd Armored Division) at the time of Operation *Cobra*. Herkness was born on April 1, 1915, in Manila, in the Philippines. His father was a US Army engineer officer, and graduate of the 1909 class of the US Army's Military Academy at West Point. Herkness followed in his father's footsteps, and graduated with the class of 1939 at West Point. He initially served in the 2nd Cavalry and after graduating from Cavalry School at Fort Riley, Kansas, in 1941, he was assigned to the 2nd Armored Division. He initially served as the executive officer of the 3rd Battalion, 66th Armored Regiment, and was promoted to captain in 1942. He served with the division during the Operation *Torch* landings in November 1942 and during Operation *Husky* in July 1943. He was promoted to major in 1943 and served as Assistant Chief of Staff, G-3 (Operations) starting on November 23, 1943. He was promoted to lieutenant colonel in the spring of 1944 and given command of the 2nd Battalion, 66th Armored Regiment.

For Operation *Cobra*, his battalion formed one of the two task forces of CCA, 2nd Armored Division, consisting of his own battalion and elements of the 22nd Infantry Regiment plus supporting arms. During the advance on July 26, 1944, he led the battalion from a command tank. That evening at about 2000hrs, his tank was knocked out along the road south of Canisy. He switched tanks with another officer and continued south with D/66th Armored in the lead. Two German tanks were knocked out along the road, and their burning hulks had to be pulled off the road using tow cables to expedite the column.

The identity of the burning tanks is not positive. Ritgen's old unit, 7./PzLehrRgt 130, lost two tanks in this area, and it is quite possible that these wrecks were in fact the two abandoned PzKpfw IV. Lt Col Herkness dismounted to supervise this operation and while approaching a nearby sunken road, he became involved in a close-range pistol duel with two German officers in the darkness. Herkness was wounded but felled one officer; the other German fled. Curiously enough, the memoirs of the commander of

7./PzLehrRgt 130, Leutnant Freiherr von Landsberg-Velen, also mention a pistol duel with an American in that area around the same time, and it is possible that the two incidents were the same encounter. Herkness was awarded the Distinguished Service Cross for his leadership that day. His battalion, 2/66th Armored, was awarded a Distinguished Unit Citation for its actions during July 26–August 12, 1944. Herkness remained in command of the battalion through the battle for the Siegfried Line, the Ardennes, and the battle for Germany in 1945. He returned to civilian life after the war, and died on July 20, 1998, in Philadelphia. His son, Lindsay C. Herkness III, a senior vice president at Morgan Stanley, lost his life in the attack on the World Trade Center on September 11, 2001.

US 2ND ARMORED DIVISION

The 2nd Armored Division "Hell on Wheels" was formed in 1940 as one of the first two US Army armored divisions. Its core tank formations, the 66th and 67th Armored regiments, were based on cadres from the Army's existing infantry-tank units at Fort Benning, Fort Meade (Maryland), and Fort Lewis (Washington State). Its first combat deployment was during Operation *Torch*, the landings in French North Africa in November 1942. A combat team from the 1st Battalion, 66th Armored landed as part of Task Force *Goalpost* (9th Infantry Division) to seize Port Lyautey (modern-day Kenitra) and its airport in French Morocco. There were some sharp but short encounters with Vichy French troops, including some tank fighting. Other elements of the division took part in the assault landings in other sectors including the landings at Fedala (modern-day Mohammedia). The main body of the division landed at Safi, to the southwest of Casablanca. Following the landings, the 2nd Armored Division was stationed on the Spanish–French Moroccan border because there was some concern that the Germans would transit through Spanish Morocco to attack the Allies from the west.

Later in November, two tank companies of the 67th Armored Regiment were used to support the British 78th Division at Beja in Tunisia, the first combat action by the M4 tank in US hands. Following the defeat at Kasserine Pass in February 1943, US units in Tunisia were in desperate need for replacements. Nearly a regiment's worth of troops and equipment were sent to reinforce the battered 1st Armored Division. The 2nd Armored Division was not committed to the Tunisian campaign since it was assigned to the forthcoming Operation *Husky* landings on Sicily in July 1943. Regimental combat teams took part in the initial Sicily landings, and became involved in tank fighting when Panzer-Division *Hermann Göring* launched a major counterattack against the beachhead at Gela. The division was subsequently used in a classic exploitation mission, spearheading the advance on Palermo.

Following the Sicilian campaign, the division was earmarked for the European Theater of Operations (ETO). The 2nd Armored Division arrived in the UK on

The 2nd Armored Division's combat debut was during the Operation *Torch* landings in North Africa in November 1942. Although the division was not committed to the fighting in Tunisia, many tanks and crews were sent to reinforce the battered 1st Armored Division after the Kasserine Pass debacle of February 1943, a series of clashes in which US troops suffered heavy casualties and were pushed back. Here, the crew members of a 2nd Armored Division M4A1 conduct routine maintenance on their tank.

An M4 medium-tank company of the 2nd Armored Division takes part in gunnery practice in Britain prior to D-Day.

November 28, 1943, from Sicily and was stationed at former British cavalry barracks in Tidworth on the Salisbury Plain. By this stage, the division was already combat-experienced, but training continued. Maneuvers and tank gunnery practice were conducted at the Imber and Minehead ranges. In the autumn of 1943, the US armored division underwent a major organizational change based on the lessons from the Mediterranean theater. The new "light" organization was intended to offer a better balance of the combat arms: three battalions each of tanks, armored infantry, and armored artillery. The old 1942 "heavy" configuration had six tank battalions and three each of armored infantry and armored artillery. The commander of the ETOUSA (ETO US Army), Lt Gen Jacob Devers, who had formerly headed the Armored Force in its formative years, was not happy about some of the changes. He convinced Gen Dwight D. Eisenhower that the two divisions already in Britain, the 2nd and 3rd Armored divisions, be spared from the turmoil of reorganization. As a result, both divisions deployed to Normandy as "heavy" armored divisions with six tank battalions and 390 tanks versus 263 tanks in the "light" divisions. The only reorganization was internal. The previous configuration of two medium- and one light-tank battalion per regiment was changed, with all tank battalions having the same configuration of one light-tank and two medium companies.

Owing to previous combat experience and a long training period in Britain, the 2nd Armored Division entered France in June 1944 as a well-trained formation. Its senior leadership was mostly the same as in Sicily except for the divisional commander. Lt Gen George S. Patton, Jr. wanted Maj Gen Hugh Gaffey as his executive for his new Third US Army, and so Maj Gen Edward Brooks became divisional commander in March 1944. The division departed from Portsmouth and Southampton and began landing on Utah Beach on D-Day+1: June 7, 1944.

THE STRATEGIC SITUATION

Wehrmacht forces in France in July 1944 were directed by OB West (High Command West) led by Generalfeldmarschall Günther von Kluge. There were two German field armies in Normandy. SS-Obergruppenführer Hausser's 7. Armee covered the sector opposite the First US Army to the west. Panzergruppe West (later 5. Panzerarmee) under General der Panzertruppe Heinrich Eberbach covered the British and Canadian forces in the Caen sector to the east. Hausser's forces in turn contained two corps. General der Infanterie Dietrich von Choltitz's LXXXIV. Armeekorps was the force most directly in the path of Operation *Cobra* and covered the area from the seacoast to the Vire. It included the three armored divisions mentioned earlier and several infantry divisions. Generalleutnant Eugen Meindl's II. Fallschirm-Korps was located to its east, covering from Saint-Lô to the Caen sector.

The fighting in the bocage country around Saint-Lô in early July was an attritional infantry battle intended to weaken the German forces to the point of collapse. As a result, Hausser had moved his three Panzer and *Panzergrenadier* divisions into the main line of resistance. This violated German tactical doctrine since the defensive mission of Panzer divisions was to remain in reserve to serve as a fast-moving counterattack force. Kluge was aggravated that Hausser had tied down his only mobile forces, making this front very susceptible to a breakthrough in the event that the brittle crust of defenses was overcome. In the event, Kluge was preoccupied by the relentless British and Canadian attacks around Caen, and like Hausser, tended to underestimate the US Army. Gen Bernard L. Montgomery had launched yet another major tank offensive, Operation *Goodwood*, on July 18. The pressure in this sector continued when the

OPPOSITE An overview of Operation *Cobra*, July 25–29, 1944.

44

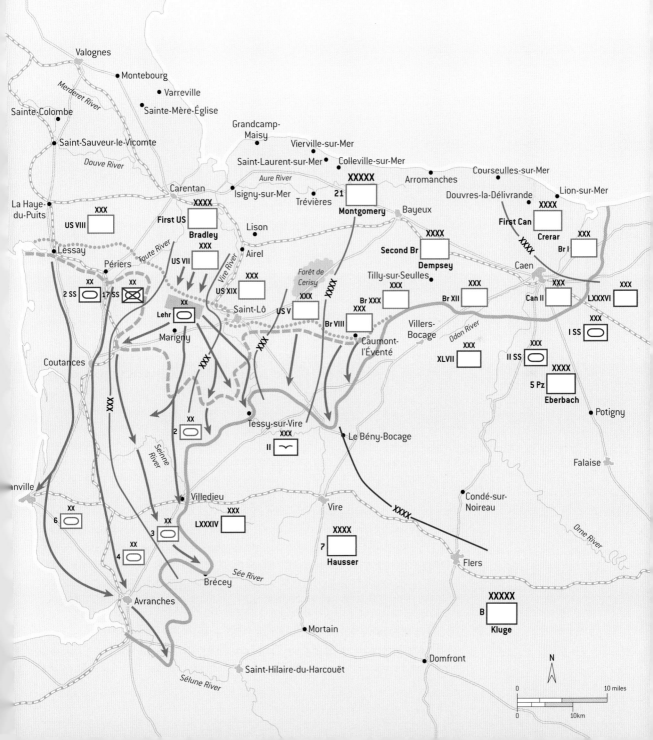

ENGLISH CHANNEL

Cherbourg

Valognes

Montebourg

Varreville

Sainte-Mère-Église

Sainte-Colombe

Saint-Sauveur-le-Vicomte

Merderet River

Douve River

Grandcamp-
Maisy

Vierville-sur-Mer

Saint-Laurent-sur-Mer

Colleville-sur-Mer

Courseulles-sur-Mer

Arromanches

Douvres-la-Délivrande

Lion-sur-Mer

Aure River

Isigny-sur-Mer

Trévières

Bayeux

XXXXX
21
Montgomery

XXXX
First Can
Crerar

XXX
Br I

La Haye-
du-Puits

Carentan

Lison

XXX
US VIII

XXXX
First US
Bradley

XXX
US VII

Airel

Taute River

Vire River

Second Br
Dempsey

Caen

XXXX
Dempsey

Tilly-sur-Seulles

XXX
Br XII

XXX
Can II

XXX
LXXXVI

Lessay

Périers

XX
2 SS

XX
17 SS

Coutances

XX
Lehr

Marigny

Saint-Lô

XXX
US XIX

XXX
US V

Forêt de
Cerisy

XXXX

XXX
Br XXX

XXX

Br VIII

Caumont-
l'Éventé

Villers-
Bocage

Odon River

XXX
XLVII

I SS

II SS

XXXX
5 Pz
Eberbach

Potigny

XX
2

Tessy-sur-Vire

XXX
II

Le Bény-Bocage

Falaise

Granville

XX
6

XX
3

LXXXIV

XXX

Villedieu

Vire

Condé-sur-
Noireau

Orne River

XX
4

Seinne
River

Sée River

Brécey

XXXX
7
Hausser

Flers

Avranches

Mortain

XXXXX
B
Kluge

Saint-Hilaire-du-Harcouët

Domfront

Sélune River

N

0   10 miles

0   10km

One of the new M4A1 (76mm) tanks of the 2nd Armored Division is shown breaking over the top of a hedgerow near Pont-Hébert during the opening phases of Operation *Cobra*. A total of 102 of these were split evenly between the 2nd and 3rd Armored divisions when first delivered on July 22, 1944.

Canadian First Army launched Operation *Spring* on the morning of July 25. Kluge remained focused on this sector of the Normandy battlefield on the presumption that it was the Allied *Schwerpunkt* (focal point), and he neglected the American threat near Saint-Lô. In response to Kluge's complaints, Hausser made a token gesture of moving back two *Das Reich* tank companies as a mobile reserve. 7. Armee headquarters did not anticipate Operation *Cobra* since their signals intelligence exploitation of US Army radio traffic was poor. There was little appreciation for the size or intentions of the opposing American force. In contrast, Allied intelligence had an excellent appreciation of German deployments and on July 24 intercepted a detailed order of battle that was decrypted by the Ultra intelligence service.

By late July 1944, Allied intelligence assessed the German defenses to be weak enough for a breakthrough operation. The intention was to carpet-bomb the German main line of resistance, and then overrun these positions with three infantry divisions, supported by separate tank battalions. Once the breakthrough was secured, the 2nd and 3rd Armored divisions would pass through the infantry to conduct a breakout. Besides the initial mission by VII and XIX Corps in the Saint-Lô sector, VIII Corps on the coast was prepared to execute a second breakout aimed at Avranches using the newly arrived 4th and 6th Armored divisions. The First US Army had a substantial superiority over German forces in this sector in terms of troops, tanks, and firepower.

A pair of M4A1 tanks of F/66th Armored at the start of the 2nd Armored Division's attack on July 26, 1944. This photograph shows several of the features adopted for the operation, including the Culin hedgerow cutters on the bow, the use of air identification panels on the engine deck of the tanks, and the use of olive drab and black camouflage paint.

Besides the initial carpet-bombing, the Ninth Tactical Air Force would provide "Armored-column-cover" over the lead tank columns using fighter-bombers to provide immediate air support against any surviving German strongpoints.

Operation *Cobra* was scheduled to begin at 1300hrs on July 24, 1944, with the heavy-bomber attack. Owing to the weather over the battlefield being heavily overcast, the air attack was canceled late in the morning. Some aircraft did not receive the recall command and bombed anyway. The main attack was postponed to the following day. Panzer-Lehr-Division weathered the first air attack with modest casualties, about 350 men and ten armored vehicles. The division's commander, Fritz Bayerlein, was convinced that his forces had repulsed a major US attack. In anticipation of more fighting, he ordered his forward outpost line from positions north of the Périers–Saint-Lô highway to withdraw south of the road where they would be less vulnerable to US artillery. This placed them immediately inside the most intense sector of the bomb zone the next day.

At the time of the initial carpet-bombing attack on July 24, Panzer-Lehr-Division held a frontage about 5km wide from the Losquette River in the west to Hébécrevon in the east. The forward defenses consisted of PzGrLehrRgt 901 in the western sector up to the Terrette River, and PzGrLehrRgt 902 to the east. FJR 14 began to reinforce the left flank. Armored support for the two sectors initially consisted of the surviving PzKpfw IV of II./PzLehrRgt 130 in the eastern sector around Hébécrevon, and PzJgLehrAbt 130 in the western sector. The second line of defense, dubbed the Yellow Line, was created along the Saint-Lô–Coutances railroad line, about 7km to the rear, followed by the Red Line near the Soulles River. On the night of July 24, the tank support for PzGrLehrRgt 902 was rotated, with the 12 PzKpfw IV tanks of II./PzLehrRgt 130 being withdrawn about 9km to the rear to the village of Dangy, while the 16 Panther tanks of I./PzRgt 6 took their place in the vicinity of Hébécrevon.

COMBAT

OPERATION *COBRA* BEGINS

The air attack on July 25 started at 0936hrs with strafing runs by P-47 fighter-bombers along the northern edge of the bomb zone. They were followed by 1,495 B-17 and B-24 heavy bombers in several waves, dropping 3,370 US tons (3,055 metric tonnes) of bombs into an area 7,000yd (6,400m) long and 2,500yd (2,285m) wide. A further 380 B-26 medium bombers completed the attack, bringing the grand total to 4,700 US tons (4,265 metric tonnes) of bombs. The effect on the German defenses was devastating. Of the 3,600 troops under Panzer-Lehr-Division's immediate control, about 1,000 were killed or wounded in the bombing attack, and at least as many severely dazed. The German communications network, which depended heavily on field telephones, was completely disrupted. The bombing coverage was erratic. The damage was worse in the center of the bomb zone where the heavy bombers had struck, while some defensive positions closer to the American lines, including about half the Panther tanks, went unscathed.

The VII Corps infantry attack began at 1100hrs with the immediate objective of seizing the crossroad towns of Marigny and Saint-Gilles about 5km from the start line. The western portion of the attack by the 9th Infantry Division bogged down quickly in the sector east of Panzer-Lehr-Division, held by elements of 5. Fallschirmjäger-Division that had not been heavily bombed. In the center, the 8th Infantry Regiment (4th Infantry Division) was supported by the 70th Tank Battalion. One infantry battalion encountered a defensive position but bypassed it; it reached the area east of La Chapelle-en-Juger by nightfall. The other battalion was stymied by a defensive position of PzGrLehrRgt 901 holding an orchard north of the Périers–Saint-Lô road,

 OPPOSITE Operation *Cobra* day by day.

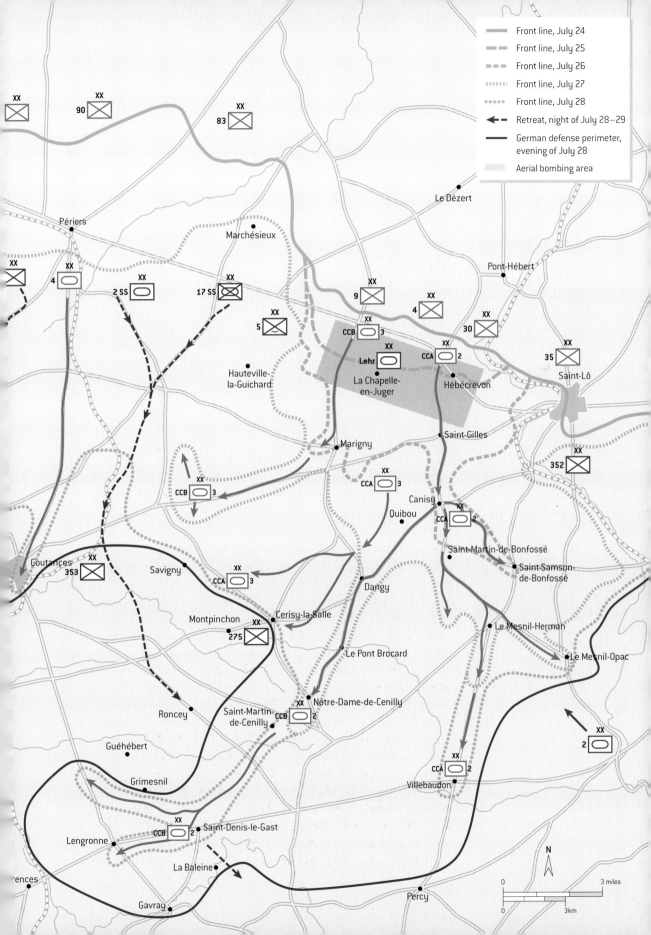

Legend

Front line, July 24
Front line, July 25
Front line, July 26
Front line, July 27
Front line, July 28
Retreat, night of July 28–29
German defense perimeter, evening of July 28
Aerial bombing area

Le Dézert

Périers

Marchésieux

Pont-Hébert

XX
90

XX
83

XX

XX
4

XX
2 SS

XX
17 SS

XX
9

XX
4

XX
30

Saint-Lô

XX
5

XX
CCB 3

XX
Lehr

XX
CCA 2

XX
35

Hauteville-la-Guichard

La Chapelle-en-Juger

Hébécrevon

Saint-Gilles

XX
352

Marigny

XX
CCB 3

XX
CCA 3

Quibou

Canisy

XX
CCA 2

Coutances

XX
353

Savigny

XX
CCA 3

Dangy

Saint-Martin-de-Bonfossé

Saint-Samson-de-Bonfossé

Montpinchon

Cerisy-la-Salle

Le Pont Brocard

Le Mesnil-Herman

XX
275

Le Mesnil-Opac

Roncey

Saint-Martin-de-Cenilly

XX
CCB 2

Notre-Dame-de-Cenilly

XX
2

Guéhébert

XX
CCA 2

Villebaudon

Grimesnil

Lengronne

XX
CCB 2

Saint-Denis-le-Gast

La Baleine

...ences

Gavray

Percy

N

0   3 miles

0   3km

but the resistance ended when the 18 M4 medium tanks arrived on the scene and blasted the orchard. After crossing the road, the battalion encountered another defense point from PzGrLehrRgt 901 supported by three Panther tanks in a sunken road. The US battalion had again become separated from the supporting tanks, and so attacked the defense point with an enveloping attack, managing to knock out two Panthers with close-range bazooka fire. The M4 medium tanks arrived, and subdued the remaining defenders.

The unlucky 30th Infantry Division had been struck by both the American preliminary bombardments, and suffered 152 casualties on July 24 and a further 662 on July 25. Two of its regiments attacked. The lead 120th Infantry Regiment ran into a German defense strongpoint supported by three surviving Panther tanks shortly after leaving the line of departure. They were supported by the M5A1 light tanks of D/743rd Tank Battalion. They began firing at the Panthers, and one was heard over the radio to exclaim "Good God! I fired three rounds and they all bounced off!" Eventually, one of the Panthers was hit by artillery fire and two withdrew southward. As the infantry continued to advance, A/743rd Tank Battalion arrived on the scene. One M4 tank was knocked out by Panther fire from farther down the road and another damaged. The company commander, Lt Ernest Aas, dismounted and hunted out the Panthers on foot. One was found west of the road to Saint-Gilles and knocked out. Aas recommended proceeding down the west side of the road which seemed to have fewer mines and defenses. No fewer than five Panthers were encountered of which one was knocked out. It should be noted that US Army identification of German tanks was often poor, and that some of the tanks identified as Panthers may in fact have been PzKpfw IV. The remaining German tanks withdrew to some nearby woods. In total, the company claimed four German tanks knocked out for the day. The neighboring 119th Infantry Regiment encountered German infantry defenses from Kampfgruppe *Kentner* (275. Infanterie-Division), as well as a handful of dug-in German tanks around Hébécrevon supporting Kampfgruppe *Heintz*.

The Rhino hedge-busters proved very successful in their use with the separate tank battalions. An after-action report by the 3rd Armored Group related that:

The rhinos churned through the enemy to a depth of 300 to 600 yards [275–550m] and returned without a single casualty due to enemy action. Interrogation of the prisoners

taken later indicated that the sortie had considerable shock action; the enemy was evidently unprepared for an onslaught of this type. In many instances the enemy relying on the thick hedgerows for protection, were ground under the tanks as they smashed through the hedgerow after hedgerow, while others were buried in their slit trenches … It was a bad time for the Nazis; their front lines were a shambles … After breaching the static enemy defenses and creating as much shock and damage as possible, the rhinos would return to the line of departure and repeat the attack as part of the infantry-tank team. Employment of the rhinos in this controlled-stampede fashion [exploited] the rhinos to their fullest extent and effected maximum surprise.

UNLEASHING THE ARMORED DIVISIONS

The infantry advance on July 25 had not reached its terrain objectives and had not secured a breakthrough. However, Maj Gen Joseph L. Collins, commanding VII Corps, felt that it had accomplished its mission in breaking the crust of the German defenses. German units invariably staged counterattacks to regain lost ground, yet the German response to the American attacks on the first day of the offensive had been feeble. In conjunction with US Army intelligence assessments of German strength in the sector, Collins concluded that the German defenses had collapsed. US tactical doctrine insisted that armored divisions should not be employed until the infantry had secured a breakthrough through the main line of resistance. Their role was to exploit the breakthrough, not to waste their resources securing it. Collins judged that the time was ripe to exploit the weakness in the German defenses.

An M4A1 (76mm) of D/66th Armored, CCA, 2nd Armored Division named *Duke* carries riflemen from the 22nd Infantry Regiment into action at the start of Operation *Cobra*.

The 2nd Armored Division was assigned to push through the Panzer-Lehr-Division defenses, while the neighboring 3rd Armored Division was assigned to push through the German defenses farther west towards Marigny.

The 2nd Armored Division mission on July 26 involved only one of its three combat commands. Combat Command A (CCA) began moving to its line of departure after midnight. CCA was based around a tank regiment from the 2nd Armored Division, a reinforced infantry regiment called a regimental combat team (RCT) from the 4th Infantry Division, and associated combat units of the 2nd Armored Division. The 22nd RCT included the 22nd Infantry Regiment, the 44th Field Artillery Battalion (SP) with M7 105mm HMC self-propelled howitzers, a medical company, and two truck companies.

Combat Command A (Brig Gen Maurice Rose)
66th Armored Regiment (Col John H. Collier)
22nd RCT, 4th Infantry Division (Col Charles Lanham)
14th Armored Field Artillery Battalion
Cos A & C, 17th Armored Engineer Battalion
702nd Tank Destroyer Battalion (less Co. B)
Co. A, 48th Armored Medical Battalion

CCA was subdivided into three battle groups, usually called task forces. Each of these was based on a medium-tank battalion carrying a company of infantry on the tanks. The 3/66th Armored (Reinforced) moved down the east side of the Saint-Gilles–Canisy road, while the 2/66th Armored (Reinforced) went down the west side. The 1/66th Armored (Reinforced) served as the command reserve and remaining units moved behind it. The composition of one of these task forces is shown below in more detail in their march order.

2/66th Armored (Reinforced) (Lt Col Lindsay C. Herkness, Jr.)

Recon Platoon, 2/66th Armored

E/66th Armored + A/22nd Infantry

D/66th Armored + B/22nd Infantry

Platoon, A/17th Armored Engineer Battalion + Platoon, 702nd Tank Destroyer
    Battalion (SP)

Assault Gun Platoon, 2/66th Armored

Mortar Platoon, 2/66th Armored

A/66th Armored + C/22nd Infantry

Panzer-Lehr-Division had very limited resources to reinforce its shattered front. At
0300hrs on July 26, the dozen surviving PzKpfw IV tanks of Ritgen's II./PzLehrRgt
130 were sent forward to reinforce various *Panzergrenadier* and infantry strongpoints
on the road north of Saint-Gilles. For example, Leutnant Freiherr von Landsberg-
Velen's 7./PzLehrRgt 130, with only four PzKpfw IV tanks, was ordered forward to
support Kampfgruppe *Scheele* (275. Infanterie-Division) in the area north of Saint-
Gilles. The available infantry reserves of 7. Armee were also sent to reinforce
Panzer-Lehr-Division, but they were very slow and were subjected to air attack during
daylight hours.

On July 26, the assault by CCA, 2nd Armored Division started at 0945hrs with a
line of departure near Hébécrevon. There was scattered resistance near the start line,
but the main factor slowing the advance was the hedgerow terrain that took time to
traverse. Only one M4 medium tank was lost in the initial advance to a German tank
or antitank gun about 365m south of the line of departure. Once the initial resistance

A headquarters jeep from the
66th Armored Regiment passes
by an abandoned or disabled
PzKpfw IV Ausf H of 8./PzLehrRgt
130 during the initial fighting on
July 26, 1944. The tank's tactical
number was 841, indicating the
lead tank of 4. Zug, 8. Kompanie.

Another view of PzKpfw IV Ausf H number 841 being inspected by troops from CCA, 2nd Armored Division on July 26.

OPPOSITE A view inside the village of Saint-Gilles after the fighting shows two of the knocked out PzKpfw IV Ausf H of 5./PzLehrRgt 130. The demolished tank in the foreground, turret number 532, was probably the one knocked out by a 500lb bomb hit from a P-47 Thunderbolt. The other tank to the left is probably the one knocked out in the duel with the Sherman tank witnessed by Lt George Wilson.

was overcome, reconnaissance units were unleashed, with companies from the division's 82nd Reconnaissance Battalion performing deep scouting for the task forces; the task forces used organic recon platoons for close-range scouting. These units typically employed jeeps, M8 armored cars, and M5A1 light tanks for these missions.

The tank/infantry columns were under sporadic mortar and artillery fire, but the first serious resistance was not met until the columns reached a strongpoint 730m north of Saint-Gilles consisting of infantry backed by four PzKpfw IV tanks of 5./PzLehrRgt 130 and a single assault gun. The lead columns called for air support and a squadron of P-47 fighter-bombers on column-cover attacked the strongpoint near the road with 500lb (227kg) bombs. The town was flanked on either side by the two lead tank/infantry teams, and entered from the northwest corner around 1500hrs. Three PzKpfw IV tanks had withdrawn into the town, and a duel ensued with the approaching M4 medium tanks.

Saint-Gilles was cleared and the columns proceeded southward toward the next road junction at Canisy. The defenses in this area included the Panther tanks of 4./PzRgt 6, but they were scattered about with no cohesive defense scheme. American reconnaissance patrols had discovered that the railroad overpass north of the town had been dropped by bombing attacks, blocking the road. As a result, the tank/infantry columns bypassed the road. The 2/66th Armored task force assaulted the town with one tank company while the other remained on a hill overlooking the town to provide overwatch coverage of the surrounding terrain. The German units in the area had no idea that the American columns had penetrated so deeply. During the advance on the town, a lone PzKpfw IV suddenly approached the road from a side road, heading north alongside a quartermaster truck column. In the confusion, the German tank commander threw a grenade into one of the 2½-ton trucks, causing numerous casualties. The Panzer careened through the column, crushing a jeep and its driver, and then sped off. On another occasion, an American MP spotted another confused German tank trying to join the column, and signaled it into position in front of an American tank which knocked it out with a shot through the rear. A German staff car attempted to pass the D/66th Armored column but was captured.

The PzKpfw IV tanks of Leutnant Freiherr von Landsberg-Velen's 7./PzLehrRgt 130 had been cut off by the American advance. The German company was ordered to counterattack around noon, but the road nearby was blocked by burned-out tanks preventing movement towards the main road; the attack was aborted. One of the company tanks was knocked out by US fire while on the security line. 7./PzLehrRgt 130 was joined by two additional PzKpfw IV tanks from 8./PzLehrRgt 130 that set up a defense strongpoint with the attached infantry. It was quite evident that the unit had been bypassed by the American advance, so after dark, the Panzers moved out to the road towards Marigny in an attempt to return German lines. Landsberg-Velen's PzKpfw IV tank broke down and was abandoned; another slipped into a crater in the road, and a third had to be destroyed by its crew after it broke down. That night, the three surviving PzKpfw IV with the infantry riding aboard finally reached Quibou and were subordinated to the Panther company there.

The town of Canisy was weakly defended and was secured by CCA, 2nd Armored Division around 1900hrs. The American columns continued to proceed southward, encountering numerous small German formations in chaotic attempts to either retreat or move to the battle front. The 2/66th Armored battalion commander, Lt Col Lindsay Herkness, lost his tank south of the town, but took command of another tank to continue the mission. A few German armored cars and half-tracks were knocked

OVERLEAF One of the first tank clashes during Operation *Cobra* occurred in the village of Saint-Gilles during the morning of July 26. A few PzKpfw IV tanks of Leutnant Lex's 5./PzLehrRgt 130 had established a strongpoint in the stone buildings around the village. The lead Sherman tank from E/66th Armored approached the town and became involved in a close-range duel with a PzKpfw IV Ausf H. One of the young infantry officers from the 22nd Infantry Regiment, Lt George Wilson, witnessed the ensuing skirmish and recalled them in his memoirs: "… from my prone position in the brick gutter, a Jerry Mark IV medium tank was cutting around the corner only a short block away and heading directly toward me. Our Sherman and the Mark IV began to fire at each other at once from point-blank range. Our tank began to back up looking for any kind of cover … Each tank fired as rapidly as possible as the distance closed to less than one hundred yards. The muzzle blasts shattered windows in the houses and storefronts, and each explosion knocked my helmet halfway off my head. The narrow, walled-in street seemed to act like a sound tunnel, and the concussion smashed at my ears … The Mark IV kept firing as it came towards us. Both tanks somehow kept missing at this close range or their armor-piercing shells were bouncing off. Finally, after an exchange of about a half-dozen rounds each, the Jerry suddenly went up in flames." Two German crewmen tried to escape but were cut down by machine-gun fire from the Sherman. The Panzer commander exited the cupola hatch, blood flowing from his ears and nose from the concussion, and in a daze, he ran forward toward Wilson. The young lieutenant fired from his hip with the three remaining rounds in his M1 rifle, and hit the Panzer commander in his leg. A second PzKpfw IV was knocked out by a Sherman in the street fighting.

out along the road. A single Panther tank was engaged around 2100hrs near the village of Saint-Martin-de-Bonfossé and knocked out by hits to its side. This proved to be a hindrance to further advance because the tank was located in a sunken road at the junction with a small stream, effectively blocking any further traffic. The Panther continued to burn and explode from an ammunition fire. It took two hours for a reconnaissance patrol to find alternate routes and for a tank dozer to arrive and push the burning tank out of the gully. By the time this had occurred, around 2300hrs, the columns were still about 3km from the objective at Le Mesnil-Herman.

With D/66th Armored in the lead, the column proceeded in the dark. The tank force reached the Le Mesnil-Herman road junction after midnight. The lead tank exploded and burned after being hit by a German antitank rocket, illuminating the crossroads in the dark. Since the objective had been reached, the columns halted for the night and began refueling and rearming with plans to secure the village after dawn. Cavalry elements moved around the German defenses and pushed to the southeast, reaching Saint-Samson-de-Bonfossé in the dark. CCA had advanced 14.5km during the course of the day, undermining Panzer-Lehr-Division's brittle defenses. Equipment losses for the day were three M4 medium tanks, a weapons carrier, and a jeep; casualties were less than 200 men. The 2/66th Armored alone had knocked out five German tanks, one assault gun, six towed antitank guns, and eight other vehicles including half-tracks and armored cars, and captured about 300 prisoners.

While CCA, 2nd Armored Division crushed the eastern wing of the Panzer-Lehr-Division defenses, CCB, 3rd Armored Division had been allotted to the 1st Infantry Division to create a similar tank/infantry battlegroup with the 18th Infantry Regiment to push through Marigny. CCB, 3rd Armored Division (Reinforced) encountered far stronger resistance in its sector, including elements of Panzer-Lehr-Division, 2. SS-Panzer-Division *Das Reich*, and 352. Infanterie-Division. The performance of CCB, 3rd Armored Division was disappointing compared to the deep advances by CCA, 2nd Armored Division. This was in large measure due to the German recognition that the American advances on July 26 suddenly threatened to cut off sizeable forces to the west of the *Cobra* battlefield, including both *Das Reich* and *Götz von Berlichingen*. Both divisions began moving forces forward on July 26 to stop the 3rd Armored Division advance short of Coutances.

US EXPLOITATION

By dawn on July 27, Panzer-Lehr-Division was no longer an effective fighting force. There were combat-capable units still in the field, but there was no divisional command network. The division had only nine tanks and six assault guns operational. Late in the evening of July 26, Bayerlein was contacted by Choltitz, the commander of LXXXIV. Armeekorps, and ordered to prepare a counterattack against the CCA spearhead near Le Mesnil-Herman the following day. He was promised a battalion of Panther tanks from 2. SS-Panzer-Division. In fact, only a company arrived and it only reached as far as Quibou before halting. The planned counterattack proved impossible. Panzer-Lehr-Division's maintenance battalion at Cerisy-la-Salle had about 30 tanks under repair. A few were hastily repaired and thrown into battle; the derelict tanks were abandoned on July 27.

The first task of CCA, 2nd Armored Division on the morning of July 27 was to secure the village of Le Mesnil-Herman. This town had been reinforced by Bayerlein during the night in anticipation of the planned counterattack. While the German forces around Le Mesnil-Herman were not strong enough to counterattack, they did provide for a stiffer defense than was anticipated. The town and its surroundings were not fully secured until 1500hrs, and three M4 tanks were lost in the process. In the midst of this fighting, A/66th Armored was detached to secure Hill 183, the high ground to the west of the Le Mesnil-Herman crossroads. By mid-afternoon, with the crossroads secure, CCA commander Brig Gen Maurice Rose formed two task forces to exploit farther south. East Task Force, based around 1st Battalion/66th Armored and two mechanized cavalry squadrons, was assigned to advance towards Tessy-sur-Vire to the southeast. It reached as far as Le Mesnil-Opac. The West Task Force, based on 3/66th Armored, the 22nd Infantry Regiment, and most of the 24th Cavalry Reconnaissance Squadron, was sent towards Villebaudon on the main road to Percy. It encountered numerous rearguards from remnants of Panzer-Lehr-Division before halting at dusk.

With the German defenses thoroughly disrupted, CCB, 2nd Armored Division, under Brig Gen Isaac White, was prepared for movement. Its mission was to advance through the gap between CCA, 2nd Armored Division and the 1st Infantry Division/3rd Armored Division team to the west. This was a classic cavalry exploitation mission, and the M5A1 light tanks and M8 armored cars of the 82nd Reconnaissance Battalion took the lead. The original plan was to use two task forces in parallel, but there was only a single viable road network and cross-country movement was too slow due to the bocage that bordered the fields along the road. As a result, the main CCB task force consisting of the 2/67th Armored and the 3/41st Armored Infantry moved down the road while two smaller groups, consisting of single tank companies teamed with a half-track infantry of the 41st Armored Infantry, proceeded on either flank.

The first roadblock was encountered at Quibou, part of the Yellow Line defenses. This had served as a collection point for German troops withdrawing the previous evening. First contact near Quibou was made by Co. A, 82nd Reconnaissance Battalion when the lead jeep was destroyed by a PzKpfw IV. A patrol from Co. B, 82nd Reconnaissance Battalion encountered two Panther tanks near the town, and one of the M8 armored cars fired several rounds of 37mm at one Panther, all of which bounced off. In the confusion, both Panther tanks drove away from the town.

An aggressive use of US reconnaissance units had a corrosive effect on German defenses. This M8 armored car of the Recon Company, 66th Armored Regiment is shown passing through La Chapelle-en-Juger as the spearhead of CCA, 2nd Armored Division in the opening stages of Operation *Cobra*.

TZF 5B TELESCOPIC GUN SIGHT

The 7.5cm KwK 40 gun on the PzKpfw IV Ausf H was aimed using the Leitz TZF 5b (*Turmzielfernrohr*) monocular telescopic gun sight. This telescope operated at a single magnification of 2.5× with a 25-degree field of view. The sight contained two engraved reticles. The center reticle consisted of an aiming triangle in the center with smaller triangles on either side. The gunner placed the target at the apex of the center triangle. This reticle provided a limited stadiametric ranging capability which allowed a well-trained gunner to estimate the range based on the size of the target compared to the large triangle. The unit of measure was a graduation (*Strich*) equaling 1m at 1,000m range with the larger triangle having sides of four graduations and the smaller triangle having sides of two graduations. Such calculations were too difficult in the heat of battle, so a gunner had to be so well trained that the procedure became instinctive. In actual practice, the gunners often used the coaxial machine gun to determine range. The series of triangles was intended to provide the gunner with a method to gauge the speed of a crossing target. The second reticle provided the graduations visible around the periphery of reticle and was used to adjust the weapon depending on the weapon and the range. In the case here, the reticle has been turned to the setting for the 7.5cm gun at a range of 200m. The two reticles were mechanically linked and by rotating the reticle, the gunner moved the center aiming reticle, forcing him to elevate the gun to compensate for range.

M55 TELESCOPE

This illustration shows the view through the M4A1 gunner's M55 telescope. This telescope operated at a single magnification of 3×. A typical set of commands by the commander to the gunner were: "Gunner … Shot (Armor-piercing) … Traverse right … Steady … On … Tank (target) … six-hundred (range of 600 yards) … Fire!" As will be noticed, the commander gave the gunner the range to target, based on observation of the target through his binoculars which included a ranging reticle, or via his periscopic sight which also included a ranging reticle. The reticle was selected depending on the ammunition in use and the ammunition type can be seen at the top. The range lines were shown in yards from 0 to 3,000yd (2,743m), with 1 indicating 1,000yd (914m), etc. The basic range of 600yd (549m) was indicated above the 1,000yd mark by the wide horizontal deflection lead lines. The gunner would elevate the gun to compensate for range. The deflection lead lines, the horizontal lines on either side of the vertical axis, are 5 mils wide on either side of the center spot, a mil representing 1yd at 1,000yd distance. The wider 60yd (55m) deflection lead line is 10 mils wide, and spaced a further 10 mils from the aiming pip. These deflection lead lines were used by the gunner to determine the amount of lead to give to a moving target.

75 - M61

An M8 75mm HMC assault gun was lost shortly afterwards farther south on the road to an emplaced German tank. With the arrival of M4 tanks of 2/67th Armored around 1100hrs, the fighting around Quibou intensified. One Panther tank covering the road was knocked out by tank fire, and the lead tank platoon found four more PzKpfw IV in a neighboring orchard, apparently abandoned, that were set ablaze by tank fire from 1/67th Armored. The columns continued through Dangy, led by the Recon Company, 67th Armored. The town was defended by about a company of infantry and a 7.5cm antitank gun. The resistance was overcome with the arrival of the M4 tanks of the 67th Armored Regiment. P-47 Thunderbolts intercepted a group of five tanks, identified as Panthers, on the outskirts of the town and claimed three.

The next major town on the road, Le Pont Brocard, was part of the second Red Line defenses on the Soulles River and was defended by a *Kampfgruppe* consisting of two understrength companies of PzGrLehrRgt 901, the remaining troops of Panzer-Pionier-Lehr-Bataillon along with a few antitank guns and 8.8cm Flak guns. This defense line was overrun around 1630hrs. Bayerlein and the divisional command post were located near the edge of the woods east of Pont-Brocard using a mobile command bus. The headquarters was bypassed by M5A1 light tanks and the staff fled to a neighboring apple orchard where the HQ radio section was located. In frustration, Bayerlein sent out a bitter radio message to corps headquarters: "After 49 days of fierce combat, the Panzer Lehr Division is finally annihilated. The enemy is now rolling through all sectors, from Saint-Gilles to the south. All calls for help have gone unanswered because no one believes the seriousness of the situation."

The American mechanized cavalry units reached Notre-Dame-de-Cenilly by nightfall. There were numerous mechanized patrols further afield, but the countryside was "Indian country" with large numbers of fleeing German troops.

NIGHT BATTLE

The advance by CCB, 2nd Armored Division on July 28 had been matched by a parallel advance of CCB, 3rd Armored Division along the road to Coutances. The rapid progress of both divisions prompted the decision of Lt Gen Omar N. Bradley, First US Army commander, to unleash two more armored divisions southward. The 6th Armored Division headed from Lessay, and the 4th Armored Division from Périers. There was every expectation that their advance would be quick as well. Signals intelligence made it clear that LXXXIV. Armeekorps was in complete disarray.

In anticipation of the actions by these two new armored divisions, the planned objectives of both the 2nd and 3rd Armored divisions were constrained on the afternoon of July 28 since it was expected that the German units trapped between the advancing armored divisions would inevitably be forced into a desperate retreat. This would most likely occur in the corridor through which 2nd and 3rd Armored divisions would be advancing on July 28. As a result, CCB, 2nd Armored Division was warned not to overextend itself. Instead of heading all the way to the coast, it was instructed to push to Saint-Denis-le-Gast and Lengronne and set up defenses. In the meantime, the neighboring CCA, 2nd Armored Division was instructed to push to the south towards Percy via Villebaudon and to the southeast towards Tessy-sur-Vire. German reinforcements were pouring into this sector in a vain attempt to halt the American breakthrough toward the east.

Command and control of LXXXIV. Armeekorps had become nearly impossible on July 28 due to the destruction of Panzer-Lehr-Division. Telephone networks had been severed and radio networks were badly disrupted. German commanders were obliged to use runners or to travel themselves. American patrols were penetrating deep behind German lines, often in the most unexpected of locations. That afternoon, SS-Obersturmbannführer Christian Tychsen, commander of 2. SS-Panzer-Division, was traveling in a Volkswagen Kübelwagen near the Haut Vents crossroads to meet with SS-Standartenführer Otto Baum, commander of 17. SS-Panzergrenadier-Division, over plans to withdraw. The Kübelwagen was ambushed by a patrol of A/41st Armored Infantry, and Tychsen was killed.

One of the US tactical innovations during the opening phases of Operation *Cobra* was to carry a squad of infantry aboard the tanks to facilitate tank–infantry cooperation. This particular M4 of I/33rd Armored (3rd Armored Division) was lost on August 9, 1944, when hit by German gunfire that started an ammunition fire.

Choltitz sent his chief-of-staff to 2. SS-Panzer-Division to coordinate the planned retreat. With Tychsen absent, command of both divisions fell to Baum. Choltitz wanted *Das Reich* along with the surviving remnants of 17. SS-Panzergrenadier-Division to withdraw down the coast towards Bréhal to avoid running the gauntlet of the 2nd and 3rd Armored divisions. By this time, both divisions had been compressed into a shrinking pocket around Roncey. However, 7. Armee commander Hausser changed the instructions at 1900hrs. He insisted that the withdrawal take place to the southeast, converging on Percy, on the presumption that these forces could be coordinated with a planned counterattack by XXXVII. Panzerkorps against the 2nd Armored Division spearhead. Hausser notified the OB West headquarters of his instructions around 2100hrs. OB-West commander, Günther von Kluge, was infuriated by this imprudent decision since it would force the retreating German forces to cross through American lines to reach Percy. He hurriedly sent a courier to Choltitz's headquarters to reverse Hausser's instructions, but by the time he arrived around midnight, the retreat was already under way.

The senior American commanders expected that the Germans would try to break out of the encirclement that night, and warned their outposts. Forward patrols were withdrawn into Saint-Denis-le-Gast. To preempt any attack on Notre-Dame-de-Cenilly, a force under Lt Col Harry Hilliard of 3/67th Armored headed to the northwest to engage German forces in the area. After a number of skirmishes, the US force withdrew back into the town at 2200hrs to protect the CCB headquarters.

2. SS-Panzer-Division had already planned its withdrawal and considered Hausser's late-arriving changes to be "incomprehensible." SS-PzGrRgt 4 *Der Führer* ignored

An M7 105mm HMC of B/78th AFAB filmed on July 26, 1944, at the start of Operation *Cobra*. This battery was in the thick of the fighting on the nights of July 27/28 and 28/29 in the vicinity of Saint-Denis-le-Gast.

Hausser's order since the unit was already in movement. The regiment headed to the south as originally planned via Granville and Beauchamps, accompanied by II./SS-PzArtRgt 2. This was the only part of the division that escaped largely intact; Baum accompanied this column. The withdrawal was aided by the predawn fog. Under the original plans, SS-PzRgt 2 along with the surviving paratroopers of FJR 6 and the engineers of SS-PiBtl 17 were to spearhead another breakout attempt to the southeast. However, Hausser's orders changed the direction of this attack. SS-PzGrRgt 3 *Deutschland* recognized that the most direct route to the concentration point at Gavray was through the village of Saint-Denis-le-Gast and a preliminary reconnaissance found that it was lightly held. The fighting began around 0400hrs, July 29 when a column ran into an outpost of E/67th Armored teamed with I/41st Armored Infantry southwest of Notre-Dame-de-Cenilly near the junction of routes D 58 and D 610 and the hamlet of La Riverie. US G-2 reports later concluded that it was made up primarily from the divisional reconnaissance battalion, SS-PzAufklAbt 2, supported by an assortment of armored vehicles from other divisional units. A few hundred dismounted German troops attempted to infiltrate the crossroad defenses followed by a column of about 30 tanks and armored vehicles. To further add to the confusion, scout elements of the 41st Armored Infantry were withdrawing into the outpost in the dark at the same time. The defending troops began with small-arms fire, but the tanks held their fire until the German mechanized column was only about 6m from the lead tank. Flares were fired and the M4 medium tanks began engaging the German column. The German battle group attempted to flank the outpost but as dawn broke, they were subjected to 488 rounds from the 78th AFAB (Armored Field Artillery Battalion) and forced back towards Roncey. The fighting ended with 17 German troops dead and 150 taken prisoner; US casualties were about 50 along with a tank and half-track. The 1/67th Armored sent a small detachment to a hill top overlooking the area where the Germans had retreated and a forward observer from 78th AFAB directed another 384 rounds against these concentrations.

In parallel, SS-PzAufklAbt 2 spearheaded another attempt to break through American lines near the crossroads of routes D 27 and D 38 near La Pinetière and Saint-Martin-de-Cenilly. PzKpfw IV tanks of SS-PzRgt 2 overran a company from the 8th Infantry Regiment (4th Infantry Division). Some US riflemen retreated back into the nearby positions of the 78th AFAB and warned the artillerymen. On hearing the firing, the battalion moved the four M7 105mm HMC self-propelled howitzers of Battery B forward to the crossroads with instructions to prepare for direct fire. In a close-range melee, the lead PzKpfw IV was hit by a succession of 105mm rounds and blown apart. The rest of the German column was taken under fire by the battalion along with four M10 3in GMC of the 2nd Platoon, Co. C, 702nd Tank Destroyer

Battalion. The German tanks tried to flank the battalion, but the M7 105mm self-propelled guns of the other batteries maneuvered to get clear fields of fire against them. During the 30-minute firefight, CCB, 2nd Armored Division was informed of the fighting. The battalion called for a divisional "Stonk," a concentrated barrage by all divisional artillery. The first Stonk landed about 450m north of the 78th AFAB positions; it was followed by two more Stonks. A small force from 1/67th Armored and 41st Armored Infantry Regiment passed through the 78th AFAB positions to push back the German force. The column withdrew, leaving seven PzKpfw IV tanks and 126 dead troops within 900m of the battalion positions. SS-PzAufklAbt 2 made yet another attempt to find an outlet, sending a patrol to the southeast near Lengronne. It did not arrive until after daybreak and by then Allied airpower had intervened.

During the morning of July 29, US fighter-bombers struck the trapped *Das Reich* columns around Roncey. These two Panzerjäger 38(t) Marder III, presumably from SS-PzJgAbt 2, were destroyed near the town church in Roncey.

There was an attempt by German units near Gavray to keep open the escape route through Saint-Denis-le-Gast, but German troops were finally forced out of the town around 1230hrs. Large groups of German troops had already infiltrated past the US outposts on foot in the fog and dark, but their failure to retain any of the key road junctions left the bulk of the motor vehicles of 2. SS-Panzer-Division and 17. SS-Panzergrenadier-Division trapped in a gigantic traffic jam on the narrow country roads around Roncey. As the morning fog lifted, the congested roads were a prime target for both aircraft and artillery. Many of the vehicles were low on fuel, further complicating the retreat. After daybreak on July 29, P-47 Thunderbolts of the 405th Fighter Group arrived to discover a "fighter-bomber's paradise" of about 500 vehicles tangled together. From mid-afternoon to nightfall, the fighter-bombers pummeled the columns. A total of 122 tanks, 259 other vehicles and 11 artillery pieces were later found destroyed or abandoned in the Roncey pocket. A separate strike by British Typhoons near La Baleine outside the pocket to the south knocked out nine tanks, eight other armored vehicles, and about 20 vehicles.

CCB, 2nd Armored Division spent most of July 29 reinforcing the various roadblocks and outposts to keep the Germans in a trap. Even though this sector was not especially active during the day, the Germans were further compressed into the Roncey pocket by the advance of CCA, 3rd Armored Division past Montpinchon on the north side of the pocket. The German commanders considered shifting the escape westward towards the coast, but these hopes were dashed when CCB, 4th Armored Division plunged south from Coutances on the west side of the pocket, finally completing the encirclement of the Roncey pocket late on July 29 when it reached Cérences and Lengronne on the Saint-Denis-le-Gast road.

THE FINAL US BREAKOUT

To no one's surprise, the Germans made a final attempt to break out of the Roncey pocket on the night of July 29/30. For a second night, there was a series of desperate close-quarter battles after darkness fell. The first major German attack occurred around 2200hrs directly toward Saint-Denis-le-Gast. At the lead of the column was a self-propelled gun which fired flares to initiate the attack. Another column led by a Panther tank overran the 3/67th Armored command post, which was located outside the town in the path of the attack. A battalion of German infantry followed and overran US positions in the graveyard on the outskirts of the town. The town defenses included the 2nd Platoon, A/67th Armored with M5A1 light tanks. They were confronted inside the town with Panther tanks and the light tanks pulled out of the town along with the half-track infantry. This opened up the main escape corridor that night.

The next attack occurred farther west, consisting of over 2,000 troops and about 90 vehicles that had congregated on the hills near Guéhébert. The 2/67th Armored had set up four roadblocks along this road during the day. The outpost at the base of this hill contained about 20 tanks of E/67th Armored, and I/41st Armored Infantry. To surprise the Americans, the first wave of German vehicles propelled themselves down the hill with their engines turned off to prevent their premature discovery; they proceeded southward on the D 59 road from Guéhébert. The column was spotted around 2320hrs by Sgt Hulon Whittington of the 41st Armored Infantry Regiment, who alerted the Sherman tanks; Whittington later received the Medal of Honor for his valiant actions that night. The lead vehicle, a 15cm Hummel self-propelled gun, was knocked out by tank fire that started a wild melee in the dark. The German vehicles were trapped along the road and pummeled by tank fire. Under the cover of darkness, wave after wave of German troops headed for the road southeastward toward Grimesnil and Saint-Denis-le-Gast. Artillery forward observers in the tanks began calling in fire from the 62nd and 78th AFAB which were located to the south.

E/67th Armored eventually withdrew a short distance down the Grimesnil road and set up more defensible positions. The troops of the 41st Armored Infantry clustered around the tanks to prevent German infantry with antitank rocket launchers from reaching the tanks. An 81mm mortar platoon deployed in the forward defenses, firing a mix of WP (white phosphorus) and high-explosive rounds. The WP rounds helped to illuminate the area. When the fighting petered out around dawn, other outposts sent their tanks into the area and over 300 prisoners were taken. The German casualties in this area amounted to about 1,000 troops killed along with numerous vehicles. One of *Das Reich*'s self-propelled artillery battalions was destroyed in this encounter along with

The German breakout attempts on the night of July 28/29 prompted the 2nd Armored Division to set up strongpoints in many of the towns around the Roncey pocket. Here, a 57mm M1 antitank gun is set up on the streets of Pont-Brocard on July 29 as an M4 medium tank passes by in the background. The gun crew members wear the camouflage battledress that saw its debut during Operation *Cobra*, only to be dropped soon after due to confusion with German camouflage suits. In the background is an abandoned SdKfz 251/3 armored radio half-track of Panzer-Lehr-Division.

the regimental headquarters. US casualties were about 45 men, one damaged M4 tank, two half-tracks, and some other vehicles.

A third wave of German troops was intercepted by the outpost of the 78th AFAB starting around 0200hrs on July 30. This was another portion of the *Das Reich* force that had congregated on the Guéhébert hills but had been blocked by the fighting with E/67th Armored a few hours before. The 78th AFAB had relocated since the morning fighting and was deployed in the

On the night of July 29/30, one of the retreating *Das Reich* columns was led by this 15cm Hummel self-propelled gun named *Clausewitz* of I./SS-PzArtRgt 2 and an SdKfz 251/18 half-track. They were followed by about 90 other vehicles and 2,500 troops. The lead vehicles were hit by tank fire, causing a traffic jam that led to the destruction of the remainder of the column in a savage night battle. They are pictured here a few days later when the vehicles had been pushed off the road.

hamlet of La Chapelle on the road between Saint-Denis-le-Gast and Lengronne. American stragglers from the rout in Saint-Denis-le-Gast began making their way into the town after midnight, including at least one M10 3in GMC. A few German troops were captured near the town and interrogated. Around 0200hrs, an unidentified mechanized column pulled up immediately in front of the battalion command post in the dark. There were a few tense moments as both sides tried to determine each other's identity in the dark. Finally, the battalion intelligence officer, Capt Simard, recognized the lead vehicle as a PzKpfw IV and began firing at it at point-blank range using the .50-caliber machine gun on his half-track; he was killed in the ensuing firefight. A radio call immediately went out to begin engaging the column with the 105mm howitzers at point-blank range. After wiping out the column near La Chapelle, the US howitzers began to fire on the remainder of the German column. The dozen self-propelled howitzers fired about 700 rounds over the course of two hours, and received additional fire support from the 62nd AFAB farther down the road. The firing quieted down around daylight. The column on the road in front of the battery included about 50 dead, 60 wounded, and 197 prisoners; the burned-out vehicles included two PzKpfw IV tanks, two StuG III, two StuG IV, three SdKfz 251 half-tracks, three half-tracks towing Flak guns, and several trucks and other vehicles. Beyond the town, US graves registration units later found 1,150 dead and 96 armored vehicles and trucks. 78th AFAB losses were light; 11 killed and wounded, one M2 half-track, and four vehicles.

By daybreak, the German escape attempts were largely spent, at a cost of about 1,500 dead and 4,000 prisoners against US losses of about 100 dead and 300 wounded. The only German unit to escape largely intact was 91. Infanterie-Division, which had retreated down the coast away from the American outposts as Choltitz had originally planned. Hausser's most powerful formation at the start of *Cobra*, 2. SS-Panzer-Division *Das Reich*, had been crippled with nothing to show for its losses.

STATISTICS AND ANALYSIS

BALANCE OF FORCES

The US Army enjoyed a substantial numerical advantage in tanks over the opposing German units during Operation *Cobra*. This was due to heavy attrition suffered by German units in the previous June–July fighting and the Wehrmacht's tendency to

This PzKpfw IV Ausf H of 8./SS-PzRgt 2 was knocked out during the confused night fighting in the streets of Saint-Denis-le-Gast by an M2 half-track fitted with a 37mm antitank gun. The 37mm antitank gun could not penetrate the frontal armor of the PzKpfw IV, but it could penetrate the turret side armor; one of the tankers is pointing at the penetration point.

Operational AFV strength, divisions of 7. Armee, June–August 1944				
	PzLehrDiv	2. SS-PzDiv	17. SS-PzGrDiv	*Total*
June 10, 1944				
PzKpfw IV	98	54	0	*152*
Panther	88	78	0	*166*
Sturmgeschütz and *Jagdpanzer*	31	42	42	*115*
Total	*217*	*174*	*42*	***433***
July 1, 1944				
PzKpfw IV	36	50	0	*86*
Panther	32	26	0	*58*
Sturmgeschütz and *Jagdpanzer*	28	36	18	*82*
Total	*96*	*112*	*18*	***226***
July 23, 1944				
PzKpfw IV	15	37	0	*52*
Panther	16	41	0	*57*
Sturmgeschütz and *Jagdpanzer*	10	25	10	*45*
Total	*41*	*103*	*10*	***154***
August 1, 1944				
PzKpfw IV	15	4	0	*19*
Panther	12	1	0	*13*
Sturmgeschütz and *Jagdpanzer*	20	6	0	*26*
Total	*47*	*11*	*0*	***58***

limit the flow of replacement tanks in favor of reconstituting units after the decimation in combat. In contrast, the US practice was a continual flow of replacement tanks to keep the units near their table of strength. The tables here show that the three key German mechanized divisions in Operation *Cobra* fell to 35 percent of their peak AFV strength prior to Operation *Cobra* and were further reduced to only about 13 percent of their peak strength due to losses during Operation *Cobra*.

The two charts below detail the Wehrmacht's declining tank strength in France during the summer. There were significant additions to the force immediately after D-Day, but subsequently, the flow of replacement tanks did not keep pace with losses. The dynamics of German tank losses were distorted by German accounting practices. Battle-damaged tanks were maintained on unit strength reports under the rubric of "repairable in more than 24 hours" even though they often required repairs far more extensive than could be accomplished at divisional level. These tanks were kept on unit rosters both for cannibalization of their parts and as well as the lack of resources to ship them back to Germany. They were not written off as losses until September 1944 after they had been abandoned in France; this accounts for the dramatic rise in tank losses in September.

Major German AFV losses in the West, June–September 1944

	June	July	August	September	Total
PzKpfw IV	125	149	49	610	*933*
Panther	80	125	41	540	*786*
Tiger	17	13	13	91	*134*
StuG III	27	68	98	356	*549*
Total	*249*	*355*	*201*	*1,597*	**2,402**

Major German AFV additions/replacements in the West, June–September 1944

	June	July	August	September	Total
PzKpfw IV	121	31	11	166	*329*
Panther	272	88	8	272	*640*
Tiger	48	42	14	49	*153*
StuG III	15	59	59	185	*318*
Total	*456*	*220*	*92*	*672*	**1,440**

In contrast, the US practice was to continue to feed replacement tanks to keep units near their nominal table-of-organization strength. As can be seen from the charts below, medium-tank strength remained fairly constant in the 2nd Armored Division in spite of battlefield attrition. No detailed reports were submitted for July 28–31, only summary reports.

2nd Armored Division tank strength, Operation *Cobra*

	Jul 23	Jul 28	Jul 30	Jul 31	Aug 1*	Aug 2	Aug 3
M4 (75mm)	185				171+9	165+30	170+9
M4A1 (76mm)	51				45+7	37+20	55+2
M5A1	158				151+2	142+21	158
Total	*394*	*385*	*387*	*367*	*385*	*415*	*394*

*Figures indicate operational + tanks in repair.

2nd Armored Division AFVs lost during Operation *Cobra*, July 26–31, 1944*

M4 tank	37
M5A1 light tank	8
M8 75mm HMC	4
M8 armored car	2
M2A1 half-track	6
M3A1 half-track	4
M4 81mm MMC half-track	1

*Vehicles knocked out, but repaired and returned to service not included.

Not all combat casualties are due to enemy action. *Destroyer*, an M4 tank of D/66th Armored, was temporarily put out of action on July 26 when it rolled off a country road on the outskirts of Canisy. The Culin hedgerow cutters are clearly visible on the front of the tank.

The dynamics of tank loss during the Normandy campaign varied considerably over time. Prior to Operation *Cobra*, most of the Allied and German tank losses occurred in the Caen sector where the most intense tank-versus-tank fighting took place. This is evident in comparing British and US tank losses as reflected in German tank-kill claims during the first two months of fighting in Normandy. The German kill claims were exaggerated, as is evident when comparing them to actual Allied losses. In the case of the US Army, the fighting in June and early July 1944 primarily involved the separate tank battalions being used in the infantry-support role, and not the armored divisions. Losses were low due to the relatively low intensity of tank engagements. Combat expenditures of tanks climbed markedly during Operation *Cobra* due to the massive increase in tank deployment, including four armored divisions. M4 losses during the first two months of fighting in Normandy totaled 1,141 (638 British/Canadian + 503 US) or about 67 percent of total Allied tank losses.

First US Army tank losses, June 6–August 5, 1944									
	Jun 6–16	Jun 17–24	Jun 24– Jul 1	Jul 2–8	Jul 9–15	Jul 16–22	Jul 22–29	Jul 30– Aug 5	*Total*
M4 (75mm)	129	37	21	21	75	33	79	68	*463*
M4 (105mm)	0	0	0	3	0	0	1	0	*4*
M4A1 (76mm)	0	0	0	0	0	0	12	6	*18*
M4 Dozer	0	3	4	1	2	4	0	4	*18*
M5A1	28	8	8	2	18	9	38	33	*144*
Total	*157*	*48*	*33*	*27*	*95*	*46*	*130*	*111*	**647**

German claims of Allied tank losses in Normandy, June 6–August 5, 1944			
	UK	US	*Total*
June 6–15	104	57	*161*
June 16–25	528	161	*689*
June 26–July 5	546	68	*614*
July 6–25	279	268	*547*
July 26–August 5	478	282	*760*
Total claims	*1,935*	*836*	**2,771**
Actual losses*	1,042	647	1,689
Actual figure is based on British/US records.			

Allied claims of German tank losses, D-Day to August 1944						
	PzKpfw III	PzKpfw IV	Panther	Tiger	Unidentified	*Total*
First Canadian Army	0	16	13	10	0	*39*
Second British Army	12	211	249	122	260	*854*
First US Army	0	82	34	27	52	*195*
Total	*12*	*309*	*296*	*159*	*312*	**1,088**
US claims through August 6; Canadian through August 11; British through August 12.						

TANK TECHNICAL EFFECTIVENESS

The popular perception of World War II tank combat imagines large-scale tank-versus-tank clashes akin to the battles in the open desert of North Africa or the steppes of Russia. This is reinforced by popular computer games such as *World of Tanks* which focus entirely on tank-versus-tank skirmishes. In spite of these popular perceptions, the vast majority of tank actions in 1944 did not involve tank-versus-tank but were more likely to be tanks against troops, buildings, vehicles, and other objectives.

In spite of the large number of tanks involved in Operation *Cobra*, tank-versus-tank encounters were sporadic and small-scale as is evident in the account above. The Normandy bocage presented much more claustrophobic terrain conditions than in other theaters and relatively short fields of fire. As often as not, tank-versus-tank engagements involved very small numbers of tanks, usually fewer than five on either side. Very little statistical evidence from wartime operational research was collected regarding tank-versus-tank fighting in Normandy. The detailed studies that do exist, such as Frédéric Deprun's recent study of the fate of the Panther battalion of 116. Panzer-Division in Normandy in July–August 1944, offer clear evidence of the small scale of the day-to-day tank fighting in Normandy. While the vast American superiority in the number of tanks undoubtedly contributed to the success of Operation *Cobra* at an operational level, the fivefold American advantage in tanks was seldom present in the numerous tank-versus-tank skirmishes.

A German assessment based on the reports of five Panzer and *Panzergrenadier* divisions indicates that AFVs accounted for about 54 percent of the kills against Allied tanks, artillery with 26 percent, and infantry antitank weapons with 20 percent. Since infantry divisions were not included in this tally, it is undoubtedly skewed towards AFVs.

German kill claims versus Allied tanks by weapon type, June 6–July 3, 1944

	Quantity	Percent
Tanks	227	42.3
Sturmgeschütz and *Panzerjäger*	61	11.4
Antitank and Flak guns	105	19.5
Field artillery	36	6.7
Close-combat weapons	108	20.1
Total	*537*	*100.0*

Postwar research of Allied tank casualties in World War II concluded that gunfire was the principal cause of tank losses, amounting to 54 percent, followed by mines (20 percent) and accidents/breakdowns (13 percent each). In the case of the US Army in the ETO in 1944, the figures were somewhat different with gunfire accounting for the greatest proportion of losses (48 percent) alongside accidents/breakdowns (20 percent), mines (16 percent), and antitank rockets (12 percent); the other 4 percent being attributed to miscellaneous causes. In the Operation *Cobra* sector, there were about 90 German antitank guns versus about 155 tanks including those in the infantry divisions. A rough extrapolation from these figures suggests that US tank losses in Operation *Cobra* might be attributed to German tanks (34 percent), antitank guns (20 percent), mines (16 percent), and antitank rockets (12 percent), with the remaining 18 percent succumbing to other, miscellaneous causes such as accidents, breakdowns, and so on.

After World War II, Britain's Army Operational Research Group (AORG) attempted to calculate the technical effectiveness of tanks in tank-versus-tank engagements using both theoretical parameters and data collected from the 1944–45 campaigns. Effectiveness was defined as "the reciprocal of the number of tanks required per enemy tank to achieve parity in battle." A summary of the results is contained in the chart below. The data suggests that the PzKpfw IV Ausf H was about 10 percent more efficient that the normal 75mm Sherman, and about 10 percent less efficient in battle than the Sherman 17-pdr Firefly in an

A US D7 tractor is used to clear a road of a disabled *Das Reich* PzKpfw IV in late July 1944 while cleaning up the Roncey pocket.

engagement at 1,000yd (915m). By the study's definition, this meant that it would take 11 75mm Shermans to reach parity with ten PzKpfw IV in an engagement at 1,000yd. The study also found that the situation was reversed at a range of 1,500yd (1,375m) where the Sherman would be more effective; this was largely irrelevant in Operation *Cobra* where engagement ranges were seldom greater than 750m.

Effectiveness of PzKpfw IV Ausf H versus Allied tanks			
PzKpfw IV Ausf H	Sherman (75mm)	Sherman (17-pdr)	Cromwell (75mm)
1,000yd (915m)	1.10	0.90	1.35
1,500yd (1,375m)	0.90	n/a	1.5

The AORG analysis suggests that the M4A1 and PzKpfw IV Ausf H were very close in combat performance. Under such circumstances, performance in a skirmish depended on the quality of the crew and the circumstances of the engagement. In the case of the 66th Armored Regiment versus II./PzLehrRgt 130, crew qualities were similar, with both sides enjoying a high level of training. The German tank crews had an edge in battlefield experience, while the American crews had more prolonged and thorough training.

TACTICAL FACTORS

In view of the similarity of the tactical effectiveness of the two tanks and their crews, the most important factor in deciding the results of the skirmish were the circumstances of the engagement. The 66th Armored Regiment enjoyed significant numerical advantage over II./PzLehrRgt 130, though this seldom translated into a significant numerical edge in the various tank-versus-tank skirmishes recounted here.

Operational research about tank-versus-tank fighting in both World War II and the Korean War strongly indicates that the side which spotted the enemy force and engaged first had up to a six-fold advantage. The simplest condensation of the rule of tank fighting is "see first, engage first, hit first." Tanks in a stationary defensive position had an obvious advantage against tanks moving to contact, since the stationary tanks were more likely to spot the approaching enemy first. US operational research from tank battles in the Korean War suggest that tanks in well-prepared defensive positions enjoyed a 3-to-1 advantage against attacking tanks. However, the actual circumstances of individual skirmishes varied widely and did not necessarily correlate to which side was on the defensive at the operational level. For example, in the case of 5./PzLehrRgt 130, most of its tanks were knocked out in direct clashes with tanks of 2/66th Armored while fighting from static defensive positions. However, the neighboring 7./PzLehrRgt 130 lost only a few of its tanks in tank-versus-tank confrontations, losing most to misadventures while trying to escape the encirclement. Although the US side was on the offensive during Operation *Cobra*, many of the tank kills scored against German AFVs occurred in the night battles when US tanks were in defensive positions while German AFVs were maneuvering in an attempt to escape encirclement.

FINAL RESULTS

Tank exchange ratios are a poor measure of combat performance at the operational level. The 2nd Armored Division suffered 49 tank losses during July 26–31, while claiming 64 German tanks. While this might suggest near-parity in results, the scale of German tank losses was constrained by the paucity of their resources at the beginning of the operation. In contrast, personnel casualties provide a better suggestion of the magnitude of the calamity suffered by German units in the opening phases of Operation *Cobra*. As can be seen in the charts below, the 2nd Armored Division suffered 914 casualties while inflicting over 7,370 German casualties, an eight-fold disparity.

The crew members of an M4A1 of the 66th Armored Regiment (2nd Armored Division) prepare their tank tarp as a sleeping shelter on the evening of July 24, 1944. When close to the battle front, the crew usually slept inside or underneath the tank for safety.

2nd Armored Division casualties, Operation *Cobra*				
	Killed	Wounded	Missing	Total
CCA	70	363	36	*469*
CCB	92	284	69	*445*
Total	*162*	*647*	*105*	**914**

2nd Armored Division claims of destroyed German vehicles in Operation *Cobra*	
PzKpfw IV	29
Panther	33
Half-tracks and armored cars	138
Miscellaneous tanks	2
Miscellaneous vehicles	400

2nd Armored Division claims of German casualties in Operation *Cobra*			
	Killed	Captured	Total
CCA	1,200	950	*2,150*
CCB	1,500	3,723	*5,223*
Total	*2,700*	*4,673*	**7,373**

CONCLUSION

The battlefield performances of tanks such as the M4 and PzKpfw IV were shaped less by their technical merits and more by the broad circumstances of the battlefield. The PzKpfw IV was still an excellent tank on the 1944 battlefield, but its performance during Operation *Cobra* was undermined by the Wehrmacht's weak force structure and its poor tactical dispositions in the Saint-Lô area. The M4 was not the best tank on the battlefield in the summer of 1944, but it was technically adequate for most missions since tank-versus-tank fighting represented only a small fraction of its combat missions. The M4's automotive reliability was an essential ingredient in the ability of the US Army to exploit the Operation *Cobra* breakthrough. The large quantity of M4 tanks on hand gave the Allies a critical edge in the fighting in Normandy in the summer of 1944.

In the midst of the debacle prompted by Operation *Cobra*, Kluge struggled to put together a counterattack force, but the growing disarray in 7. Armee undermined German plans before they could be completed. Kluge shifted 2. Panzer-Division and 116. Panzer-Division from the British sector to the American sector in the hopes of containing the US breakthrough. Although the two divisions did temporarily limit the eastward advance of VII Corps and XIX Corps on July 29–30, they did not have the strength to carry out their main mission of sealing the gap. By the end of July, the First US Army had captured about 20,000 German troops and had effectively disabled the two German corps and most of their constituent divisions. Hitler attempted to counter Operation *Cobra* with the ill-conceived Operation *Lüttich* in August 1944 that intended to cut off the US Army spearheads at the sea at Avranches. This Panzer attack was stopped at Mortain by the First US Army and helped precipitate the collapse of German defenses in the Caen sector and the rout of German forces in northern France.

FURTHER READING

There is extensive published material on both the M4A1 medium tank and the PzKpfw IV, but the literature tends to focus on technical details and not on operational issues. Both the 2nd Armored Division and Panzer-Lehr-Division are well covered in published accounts. The Panzer-Lehr-Division commander, Fritz Bayerlein, was interviewed on several occasions by the US Army Center for Military History for its Foreign Military Studies program, and these reports are most readily accessible in the Spayd and Steinhardt books. Many of the recent divisional histories of Panzer units in Normandy have come out in France, and the Perrigault book remains the most thorough and detailed history of Panzer-Lehr-Division.

Besides the books and articles on this subject, I also used the after-action reports of the 2nd Armored Division and the "Combat Interview" accounts, located in Record Group 407 at the National Archives and Records Administration (NARA II) in College Park, Maryland. On the German side, Panzer-Lehr-Division records are thin, but I used other records from the microfilm Record Group 242 holdings at NARA II for 7. Armee and LXXXIV. Armeekorps. Another useful source are the "R" series reports prepared by James B. Hodgson as part of the US Army's Center for Military History official campaign account "Breakout and Pursuit." These unpublished monographs detailed the German side of the story for various chapters in the official history. They are available at NARA II as well.

This PzKpfw IV Ausf H had been displayed for many years at the Falaise museum, but in 2013, it was moved to the new Omaha Beach museum near Colleville-sur-Mer.

UNPUBLISHED MONOGRAPHS AND DOCUMENTS

E. Benn & R. Shephard (1952). "Tank Effectiveness: A Comparison of the Theoretical Measure with Observed Battle Performance." Byfleet: AORG Report No. 6/52.

Alvin Coox & L. Van Loan Naisawald (1951). "Survey of Allied Tank Casualties in World War II (ORO-T-117)." Johns Hopkins University, MD: Operations Research Office.

Forrest Creamer (1947). "Employment of Armor and Infantry, XIX Corps: 14 June–1 August 1944." Fort Knox, KY: Armored School.

H.G. Gee (1952). "A Survey of Tank Warfare in Europe from D-Day to 12 August 1944." Byfleet: AORG Memo C-6.

Donald Houston (1974). "The 2nd Armored Division's Formative Era 1940–1944." Oklahoma State University, OK: Master's Thesis.

Herbert Long (1948). "The Tank Battalion in Operation *Cobra*: 2nd Battalion, 66th Armored Regiment, 2nd Armored Division in the historic St Lo Breakthrough in July 1944." Fort Knox, KY: Armored School.

Lawson Magruder (1950). "Company G, 22nd Infantry (4th Infantry Division) in the St Lo Breakthrough 31 July–1 August 1944." Fort Benning, GA: Infantry School.

Glenn T. Pillsbury *et al.* (1950). "Employment of the 2nd Armored Division in Operation Cobra 25 July–1 August 1944." Fort Knox, KY: Armored School.

Henry Zeien (1947). "Operations of the 3d Battalion, 66th Armored Regiment in the St Lo Breakthrough." Fort Leavenworth, KS: Command and Staff College.

n.a. (1945). "Preliminary Notes: PzKw IV Mounting 7.5cm KwK 40 (L.48)." Chertsey: School of Tank Technology.

n.a. (1943). "Preliminary Report No 15: PzKw IV (Special)." Chertsey: School of Tank Technology.

US ARMY FOREIGN MILITARY STUDIES

James B. Hodgson. *The Effect of the Cobra Bombardment on Panzer Lehr Division, 24 and 25 July 1944* (R-31).

James B. Hodgson. *The Eve of Defeat* (R-57).

James B. Hodgson. *Thrust-Counter-Thrust: The Battle of France* (R-58).

Alfred Zerbel. *Bombing and Operation Cobra: Kampfgruppe Heinze (24–30 July 1944)* (A-910).

BOOKS

Mark Bando (1999). *Breakout at Normandy: The 2nd Armored Division in the Land of the Dead.* Osceola, WI: MBI.

Georges Bernage (2000). *The Panzers and the Battle of Normandy June 5th–July 20th 1944*. Bayeux: Heimdal.

Gordon Blaker (1999). *Iron Knights: The US 66th Armored Regiment*. Shippensburg, PA: White Mane.

Martin Blumenson (1961). *Breakout and Pursuit*. Washington, DC: US Army Center of Military History.

Frédéric Deprun (2011). *Panzer en Normandie: Histoire des équipages de char de la 116. Panzerdivision juillet–août 1944*. Louviers: Ysec.

Max Hastings (1981). *Das Reich: The March of the 2nd SS Panzer Division through France*. New York, NY: Holt, Rinehart, & Winston.

Donald Houston (1977). *Hell on Wheels: The 2nd Armored Division*. San Francisco, CA: Presidio.

Franz Kurowski (2011). *Elite Panzer Strike Force: Germany's Panzer Lehr Division in World War II*. Mechanicsburg, PA: Stackpole.

Eric Lefevre (1983). *Panzers in Normandy Then and Now*. London: After the Battle.

Didier Lodieu (2014). *La Big Red One face à la 2 Pz.-Div*. Louviers: Ysec.

Kamen Nevenkin (2006). *Fire Brigades: The Panzer Divisions 1943–1945*. Winnipeg: Federowicz.

Jean-Claude Perrigault (1995). *Le Panzer-Lehr-Division: Le choc des alliés brise l'arme d'elite de Hitler*. Bayeux: Heimdal.

Helmut Ritgen (1995). *The Western Front 1944: Memoirs of a Panzer Lehr Officer*. Winnipeg: Federowicz.

P.A. Spayd, ed. (2005). *Bayerlein: After Action Reports of the Panzer Lehr Division Commander from D-Day to the Ruhr*. Atglen, PA: Schiffer.

Walter Spielberger *et al.* (2011). *Panzerkampfwagen IV and its Variants 1935–1945 – Book 2*. Atglen, PA: Schiffer.

Frederick Steinhardt (2007). *Panzer Lehr Division 1944–45*. Solihull: Helion.

H.J. Stöber (1966). *Die eiserne Faust: Bildband und Chronik der 17. SS-Panzergrenadier-Division GvB*. Neckarmünd: K. Vowinckel.

Otto Weidinger (2012). *2 SS Panzer Division Das Reich, Vol. V*. Winnipeg: Federowicz.

George Wilson (1987). *If You Survive: From Normandy to the Battle of the Bulge to the End of World War II, One American Officer's Riveting True Story*. San Francisco, CA: Presidio.

Michael Winninger (2013). *OKH Toy Factory – The Nibelungenwerk: Tank Production in St. Valentin*. Andelfingen: History Facts.

M. Wood & J. Dugdale (2000). *Waffen SS Panzer Units in Normandy 1944*. Farnborough: Books International.

Steven Zaloga (2008). *Armored Thunderbolt: The US Army Sherman in World War II*. Mechanicsburg, PA: Stackpole.

Niklas Zetterling (2000). *Normandy 1944: German Military Organization, Combat Power and Organizational Effectiveness*. Winnipeg: Federowicz.

n.a. (1945). *History of 67th Armored Regiment*. Braunschweig: G. Westermann.

n.a. (1989). *History of the Second United States Armored Division 1940 to 1946*. Nashville, TN: Battery Press (originally 1946).

n.a. (1980). *Spearhead in the West: The Third Armored Division 1941–1945*. Nashville, TN: Battery Press (originally 1945).

INDEX

References to illustrations are shown in **bold**.